The Love
Exchange

D0862706

Margaret Therkelsen, a professional musician for over thirty-three years, was guided to become a counselor and retreat speaker on prayer and the spiritual life. She received her master's degree in marriage and family therapy and has a successful counseling practice.

The Love Exchange

An Adventure in Prayer

Margaret Therkelsen

Fleming H. Revell
A Division of Baker Book House Co
Grand Rapids, Michigan 49516

© 1990 by Margaret Therkelsen

Published 1998 by Fleming H. Revell
a division of Baker Book House Company
P.O. Box 6287, Grand Rapids, MI 49516-6287

Previously published by Bristol Books

Printed in the United States of America

Library of Congress Cataloging-in-Publication Data

Therkelsen, Margaret, 1934–
    The love exchange : an adventure in prayer / Margaret
Therkelsen.
        p.   cm.
    Originally published: 1st ed. Wilmore, KY : Bristol Books,
1990
    ISBN 0-8007-5660-6 (pbk.)
    1. Prayer—Christianity. 2. God—Love. 3. God—Worship and
love. 4. Therkelsen, Margaret, 1934– . I. Title.
[BV215.T44   1998]
248.3'2—dc21   97-43970

For current information about all releases from Baker Book House, visit our
web site:
                    http://www.bakerbooks.com

This book is lovingly dedicated to my dear mother who taught me to pray and to my loving husband who prays with me now. Without his strong help I could not have written this book.

Contents

Acknowledgments

Special thanks to Ruthie Snyder for the many conversations about all aspects of the spiritual journey. As we talked, the power and the beauty of the Love Exchange stood out in uniqueness and simplicity. These conversations led me to write this book about the Love Exchange.

Loving thanks also to my sister, Edith Stamper, and to two close friends, Lynn Baskin and Lois Mulcahy, for typing the manuscript.

Introduction

Putting into words my deepest experiences with God seems a rather presumptuous and frightening thing, knowing that thousands of other people have had similar experiences. But as I have shared the principles of the love exchange in prayer seminars and retreats, the response has been overwhelming. I have heard all types of responses: "I've been having that same experience, but I didn't know what to call it." "I've been wondering if a time of loving God isn't the most beneficial experience in prayer." "I've felt such love for God and have not known what to do with that love."

These responses, common to many people, prompt me to set down on paper my own experience. The frightening aspect is that I'm taking deeply personal times with God and exposing them to the public. Some experiences with him are almost too sacred to reveal.

The realization of what works for one person does not necessarily work for another has been taken into consideration. I value our individuality and temperament patterns, but the love exchange is a basic model for reaching out to God and then God responding regardless of the ingredients of our personality. That there is a mutual communion, a reciprocal time with God, is the essence of this book.

Even though hundreds of books are available on the experience of contemplation, my intent is to deal with a simple pattern for allowing God to respond. Other books do not articulate this, though they may infer a dialogue in some way. My exposure to their literature has always led me to a one-sided stance where I have no problem in loving God, but it has failed to illuminate my thinking on how to allow him to come to me. If indeed God loves me as Scripture proclaims, how do I realize this love relationship?

The simple but workable pattern the Holy Spirit has revealed to me over a period of several years might help you as it has me. God is certainly beyond patterns and plans, however I am thankful for any aids which help me know the wondrous Reality that is accessible and yearns to be friend and companion, as well as Savior and Redeemer.

My prayer is that you allow God to draw nigh to you even as you draw nigh to him—so that a Love Exchange may take place. As this Love Exchange deepens, God can have more of you than he has ever had, and your lives will be hidden in him, freely alive and transformed in his loving presence.

ဆာ•က
I know God
loves you,
but knowing myself
as I do,
it is hard to believe
he loves me.
ဆာ•က

Chapter 1

The Discovery of the Love Exchange

For this reason, I bow my knees before the Father, from whom every family in heaven and on earth derives its name, that He would grant you, according to the riches of His glory, to be strengthened with power through His Spirit in the inner man; so that Christ may dwell in your hearts through faith; and that you, being rooted and grounded in love, may be able to comprehend with all the saints what is the breadth and length and height and depth, and to know the love of Christ which surpasses knowledge, that you may be filled up to all the fullness of God

Ephesians 3:14-19

The persistent ring on our old alarm broke the silence of that spring morning eight years ago. I roused from sleep with tremendous expectation. Since returning to a daily, early morning prayer time, 6:00 to 7:00, the drawing to the place of prayer was increasing day by day. I slipped out of bed and, with anticipation that Jesus would already be there, groped my way down the hall to my prayer corner. Immediately as I sat down, I felt such love for Jesus flooding my heart. How I loved him! How good he was to me! The journey back from years of rebellion and disobedience to a life of walking with Jesus daily was due to his persistent love for me. He had been cleansing me of anger and resentment toward him and myself. He had provided me with a wonderful husband and a job. I was able to say with Joel that God truly was restoring the years the locust had eaten (Joel 2:25). The depth of my love for him was beyond anything I had experienced. Micah 7:18-20 was a joyous reality.

Early that morning there welled up within me such love for Jesus, I cold hardly contain it. What a Lord, what a Savior! I poured my love out on him in the stillness of that hour as I had been doing for months. From the depths of my soul and spirit my love, gratitude, appreciation and adoration flowed out to him in words of devotion. An awareness of time escaped me for now a total absorption in him pulled me out of the temporal and into the eternal. Loving him dominated my thoughts and saturated the air. This love was so intense I felt pain in my heart. Engulfed in an awareness of how deeply I loved him, my whole focus centered on him in a totally self-forgetful way.

I had been speaking aloud words of love to him, but words failed. With uplifted hands I called out, "Lord, you know that I love you with all my heart, all my soul, all my mind and all my energies." At the height of that moment of total loving I experienced his mighty love pouring down over me as he said, "I love you, Margaret, with an everlasting love. Though the mountains may be removed and the hills shake, my loving kindness will never be removed from you. I have you inscribed on the palm of my hand, you are precious in my sight, you are honored, and *I love you*. I am your husband and your protector."

These glorious Scriptures, God's own words to me, came sweeping over me as I received his love in body, soul and spirit. He responded in such reality. Not only did he receive my love, but he gave his love.

Pouring Out Love

This powerful and almost overwhelming response of God that day had been the result of several years of taking five to eight minutes of my daily prayer time to pour out my love on him. These seasons of love would occur sometimes at the beginning of my prayer time, sometimes at the end, never at a fixed time. They occurred at those times when my love rose up to express itself in thoughts which were allowed to flow freely. It should be said here that this response was not an emotional response but a sense of gratitude that comes from reflection on the Word and by faith. Seldom was emotion a very large part of this experience. His love was received and realized by declaring aloud the Scriptures that relayed that love to me. Slowly and thoughtfully I would repeat those Scriptures until they came alive first in my heart and then in my mind.

After reviewing the love Scriptures, of which I had quite a collection, and with my arms held high as symbol of surrender and readiness to receive his love, I would pray something to the effect, "Lord, you love me and I receive your love at this very moment. As I read your Word, I know you love me because you say you love me. By faith in your Word I reach up to receive your total and complete love for me. I receive your love now. Thank you, Jesus, for that Calvary love."

In other words, I was lingering in his presence, not only to love him but to allow him an opportunity to respond to me, in this place and at this time. By faith I believed God had given me his love, and I affirmed that by declaring aloud I had indeed received it with both joy and gratitude. This declaration came out of my own words as well as Scripture, and the offering of it brought a reality of having received his love. We live so much of our Christian lives with only a shadowy back drop of God's love. This experience was an intentional, on-the-spot affirmation of his love being received.

Days and weeks passed without any emotional response. The fact that the times of deep emotional feelings were certainly fewer than the many times I felt no emotional response did not discourage me from doing what I knew as my right and privilege if I took the Word seriously. The main issue was not the feelings involved but the reality of his love for me. The communication involved faith independent of feelings. By faith I received God's love, and by faith I believed he received my love for him. The exchange of love was taking place whether by faith or on those rare occasions accompanied by feelings, because I would leave the place of prayer with a definite sense of being loved and accepted.

Something was happening to me: As I daily received God's love in my life, as I declared his love and received it by faith, there emerged stirrings in my heart of a deepening love for him. The promise of 1 John 4:16, of how much he loves me, was starting to be a reality. "We have come to *know* and have *believed* the love which God has for us. God is love and the one who abides in love abides in God, and God abides in him." My capacity to love him was being deepened, and it was touching the well springs of deep feelings. A deep sense that we were enjoying each other would pervade my outlook. Tugging at me was a growing sense of urgency to abide in the Love Exchange all day. An unquenchable desire to deepen my understanding of his love and to please him by obeying the love commandments occupied my deepest desires. Paul's prayer for the Philippians became my prayer: "This I pray, that your love may abound still more and more in real knowledge and all discernment" (1:9).

The Discovery

That spring day, however, the reality of God's love for me poured through my body, soul and spirit, but by faith *with* feelings. His love and my love mingled and intermingled in a renewing Love Exchange. As he poured his love on me, my love for him intensified. I didn't know where my love stopped and his began. "The one who joins himself to the Lord is one spirit with Him" (1 Corinthians 6:17). I knew I was cherished and loved unconditionally, and I knew I loved him as totally as I was capable at that time. Words were left far behind, our Love Exchange was heart to heart, spirit to spirit, life to life.

This relationship was so sweet, so vivid, so over-whelming. For several minutes it was reciprocal, but such an encounter was so new to me I was unable to maintain my part very long. The sense of loving God and receiving his love lifted me into a new awareness of how deeply and eternally he loved me. The Love Exchange profoundly touched my life that day. Reluctantly I left our family room, but I knew God loved me more fully than I could ever express in my limited way. I was loved, comforted, nurtured, accepted and in touch with myself and God. I was eager to let his divine love flow through me that day. My body was refreshed and rested. I had partaken of his divine nature and allowed him permission to love me just as I am. That love strengthened me to want to love him more, to be a channel for his love and grow in his love as well.

Some dynamic truths emerged from that intense Love Exchange. First, God is lonely for our love to be poured out on him. He needs us and yearns for our loving companionship and fellowship. His desire is to express love to us in concrete ways and manifest himself as the lover of our souls. As a good heavenly Father, he offers his love to us daily.

Second, my deepest need is to know that God loves me, unconditionally and totally, that is, to know through experiencing his love that Jesus was sent for me. You see, I know God loves you, but knowing myself as I do, it is hard to believe he loves me. The Love Exchange reveals in a real way that Jesus loves *me*. As I appropriate his love by faith each day, there is a growing sense of truly *knowing* he loves me.

Knowing his love for me had been part of my experiences with God over the years. My conversion experience in grade school, my asking him to be Lord of my life in high school, the infilling of his Spirit in later years, special occasions such as a physical healing were all times I experienced his love. Each experience authenticated the fact of his love for me. Yet to meet the challenges of each day, I found I needed his love realized in my life more than at distinct, unusual times, but rather on a daily basis. How wondrous it was to begin experiencing that love daily, even the potentiality of minute by minute. Is this not the joy of our Christian walk, to appropriate this love at a definite time and place? So significant has been my daily experience of receiving his love for me and giving my love to him that I continually drink at the fountainhead the wonderful love of God. What a feast, what a banquet table! Isaiah 12:3 says, "You will joyously draw water from the springs of salvation." The Scriptures are full of such descriptions of the Love Exchange.

Day by day what a discovery to know that God desires my love, and I need his love on a daily basis. Mountaintop experiences are mileposts along our spiritual journey. As life changing as they may be, such experiences are not sufficient, for this love must be given and received regularly, day by day. Is this not what the bottom line of our time of prayer is all about? To receive God, who is love, and to pour out our love on him fills in the space between those big experiences. As we receive his love we can learn to give love to him constantly throughout the day. It is an appropriation of his everlasting love. I doubt if we can plumb the depths of his love, or drain the wellspring dry. The tragedy is that we appropriate so little of it and are content with so little. He wants us in a daily way to have fellowship together in his love.

Third, another aspect of my deep need for learning to receive God's love daily is that his love reaches down to touch the person I truly am in him. My real true self, made in his image, is the eternal self. His love coming to me by faith, through his word, encourages the person I am in him to grow into a more mature individual. My maturation depends on this love as it affirms me, just as a parent, who by being lovingly present or emotionally present to a small child, allows the true person to be accepted and nurtured. Only as I receive God's love in my spirit can I become the person he created me to be. Then can I know who I am in him.

God's love coming to my spirit daily in the Love Exchange causes me to feel good about who I am. I feel valuable and worthwhile. My sense of self-esteem, built on his esteem of me, develops as his love reveals how precious I am. As I accept his love, I learn I am a worthy person. I am accepted in the beloved (Ephesians 1:6) .

The Holy Spirit works quietly and yet dynamically deep within me as the Love Exchange is experienced. I am not always aware of what's happening deep within me. I cannot be loved by God Almighty and not be gradually changed at every level—my desires, motives, goals, my very living.

Cooperation is the key that allows his love to pervade my whole being as I respond in love to others. The alterations within my spirit may be unknown to me for months, even years, yet silently his love does transform or change everything it touches. For me the most profound change is that awakening to the whole dimension of his love being so available and the power of obeying the love commands of Jesus. This is something I cannot do unless I am receiving his love actively day by day.

Fourth, through his love God teaches me how to love him, myself and others. That love begins to flow out of me to others, those easy to love and those hard to love. The commandment "to love even as he loves us" is impossible in the realm of human—centered love, but the Love Exchange allows divine love to be utilized for others. In loving others I had been so selective, falling far short of the love commandments. I did not want to love. I felt I could say when and where I would love. Yet with this attitude I knew I had failed him, causing guilt to well up within me. As God and I loved each other in the Love Exchange, he began to teach me the utter necessity of obedience to his standards of love, regardless of my own personal feelings.

This reality caused a revolution to begin in me. Jesus never commanded anything we cannot fulfill through his grace. Therefore, this message of love and what I knew my response must be can be a reality where in our world it is very difficult to love. A whole new world began to emerge as I viewed love in a totally new perspective.

Finally, learning to love God is the transformation of my shallow, self-seeking life into his likeness, that I might be brought into his deep love (Romans 8:29).

The need for the Love Exchange is essential, letting divine love from Jesus work in me to love the Father and thus all my heart, soul and mind are unified in that loving. His love pulls us out of our narrow human love into his divine love. Only God can work such a change in us.

Intimacy is defined as the ability to give and receive love. All other intimacies are dependent on my loving God and knowing he truly loves me. We are made for communion with him so that nothing else satisfies. Then we feel confident to love others and ourselves in a redemptive way.

He needs our love. He is lonely for our loving fellowship, and we need above all other things to know that he loves us. Do we love him with all our heart, soul and mind? Do we love our neighbor as ourselves? Are we on a journey which learns to love with his love? The Love Exchange is a daily practice of maturing in giving and receiving love.

Exercise: Find a quiet place and pour out your love on God. Sit quietly and affirm his love for you by saying slowly and thoughtfully, "God so loved [your name], that he gave his only begotten Son, that [because I] believe in him [your name] should not perish, but have eternal life" (John 3:16). Affirm aloud that you receive this wondrous love today, right at this moment and thank him with enthusiasm. Return as often as you can in your heart and mind to this experience as you go through your day, by repeating quietly within yourself the ceremony of loving God and believing and receiving his love for you.

ಬಾ•ಆ

God's love
looks beyond
the present—
its blemishes,
its failings,
its weaknesses—
to what we
are destined
to become.

ಬಾ•ಆ

Chapter 2

God's Love and Its Qualities?

And we have come to know and have believed the love which God has for us. God is love, and the one who abides in love abides in God, and God abides in him.

1 John 4:16

As the warm spring sun illuminated the craggy mountain summit opposite my point of observation, my binoculars helped me focus on a majestic sight across the way. Perched on a protruding rock, a noble eagle stood guard over her nest just below. So proud, so protective, this mother bird displayed love toward her eaglets.

Now the soft, buoyant air started to roll up the side of the mountain. As I sat there I longed to ride on the currents as I had seen the eagle do in the past. As the air caressed my face I wondered if the eagle knew the same tug to fly that I experienced. Within a few moments the great eagle slipped gracefully off the perch and rode on those soft billows from the valley floor. She seemed to be communicating something to the eaglets about flight. It must have been a message of loving encouragement for the young to try their wings and experience the thrill of soaring on the currents along the mountain cliff.

Following several graceful passes in view of the eaglets, the mother perched again at the nest. Now with an aggressive approach she nudged one of the young from the nest. Instantly it struggled to remain in the security of the nest only to find itself being brushed off the ledge. Plummeting through the air the eaglet struggled to fly with little success, its untrained wings flapping vigorously while screeching for help. Where were those soft currents its mother rode on a few minutes earlier? Why was it so difficult to fly?

The mother eagle watched with a calm calculating eye, while I nearly lost my footing as I strained within to catch the flailing eaglet. Just at that moment the eagle exhibited her maternal prowess by swooping down to catch the offspring lovingly on her great wing only moments before it would have been too late. She returned the eaglet to the nest so the others might experience the same lesson in flight. And they all experienced another lesson—a lesson in love.

That day will always be my special memory. The beauty of the mountains, the majestic sight of the eagle, the soft breeze, but most of all the lesson in love. This mother eagle taught me a lesson in love I needed at that time.

Deuteronomy 32:3-13 speaks of the mighty eagle as symbolic of God and his love.

> For the Lord's portion is His people;
> Jacob is the allotment of his inheritance.
> He found him in a desert land

And in the howling waste of a wilder-
ness;
He encircled him, He cared for him,
He guarded him as the pupil of his
eye.
Like an eagle that stirs up its nest,
That hovers over its young,
He spread his wings and caught
them.
He carried them on his pinions.
The Lord alone guided him,
And there was no foreign god with
him.
He made him ride on the high places
of the earth,
And he ate the produce of the field;
And He made him suck honey from
the rock,
And oil from the flinty rock.

A mother dashes before an oncoming vehicle to snatch her baby from death, and people say, that's like God's love, self-forgetful and concerned only with the beloved.

A father risks his own life by giving blood to a son that is in need of a transfusion. That's like God's love, to keep on giving when it is harmful for the father.

A son, who has defied his parents and the laws of the land is still loved and prayed for by the mother though he continues to refuse God's love. How like God's love it is to yearn for a response and not give up.

A music teacher accepts a young person into the studio and sees the gifts and talents that are there. Then he urges the sharpening of these talents and loves that person into what she can become. That is like God's love.

The subject of God's love is one of the most profound topics in all the world. Its depth and height will probably never be fully sought out. Hundreds of volumes are dedicated to this lofty pursuit and yet not one is definitive. My purpose here is not to attempt the impossible, but to define, as it pertains to the purpose of this book, what is God's love as it relates to the Love Exchange and to list four qualities of that love. To spotlight only four qualities or facets of this magnificent diamond will be a tremendous task.

The passage in Deuteronomy 32:9-13 illustrates the qualities of significance for this presentation.

I do believe that the message of God's love, and how to appropriate that love, is the most needed message in our age. The chronic illness affecting people today is the sense of being unlovable and unlovely where God is concerned. If we do not know God loves us, then we cannot learn to love ourselves and others. Only his love in our human spirits can convey we are loved and wanted by him.

We have stressed every aspect of the godhead and human experience over the centuries, but I believe the core of the gospel has been and always will be—God loves me, just as I am. As I experience his love for me in a deeply personal way, I become a whole person, a channel for his love to flow out from me to others.

His loving others through me brings about my transformation into his image. This transformation can only be experienced by his love being shed abroad in my heart or human spirit by the Holy Spirit (Romans 5:5). This is the message of the ages—God's love must be birthed in me as a gift of love.

How do we tie down a definition of a love so holy, so unlike self-centered, self-seeking human love? I like this definition: "Divine love loves us for our highest good, with no thought of anything in return." In other words, I love you for what I can give you that is best for you.

We know human love says we love another for *our highest good*, or I love you for what I can get from you. Human love then loves only to get, while divine love loves to give, with no thought of itself or any return.

The old mother eagle was intent on caring for her babies, aiding their growth and maturity until they can soar in the high places, full and free. The concern was not for herself but the beloved offspring. The love of a mother for her babies is a common symbol of God's love.

What are the qualities of divine love?

Shared Love

One of the first qualities of God's love is that it has to be shared. Giving expression to love is a must, regardless of the response. This giving love is expressed in John 3:16, "God so *loved*, that he *gave*." By giving us his love God teaches us to love. Love does beget love. Someone who pours out selfless love gets our attention, for we are drawn into returning that love. To ignore someone who keeps on loving me no matter what I do, is very difficult.

The mother eagle keeps pouring out love, giving and giving, no matter what the eaglet does. She yearns for a response from the young birds, and so she cares for the babies by hovering over their nest. Because they are the apple of her eye, she invests a portion of herself in all stages of their development.

Years ago I had an acquaintance who was like a mother eagle to young men in prison. She visited regularly in several prisons over a long period of time, "hovering" over her children there, loving, caring and giving.

She told me a story about a young man who was so wounded because he had never known the love of a "mother eagle." His father abandoned him when he was only a child, and he found himself in one tragic situation after another. When this woman began making weekly visits to his prison, he ridiculed and scorned her love. She kept returning week after week, year after year. Several years had passed with no response from the young man. She had assured him over and over again that she loved him and was praying for him, when one day he pushed her aside saying, "I don't want your old love. Quit trying to give me something I don't want and don't need."

She replied, "I am going to keep on giving you God's love, no matter what you do or say."

He furiously stomped out of the room, and she headed down the hall to leave. As she was about to open the door, she heard running steps behind her. This young man, so starved for love and so wounded by lovelessness, threw his arms around her and with sobbing hesitation said, "Oh, I *do* need your love. I need God's love. Don't give up on me."

They wept and embraced. This young man's resistance broke after years of seeing God's love flow out to him. Such love meant the sacrifice of constancy on the woman's part.

Such is God's kind of love—giving, yearning for a response, never giving up. Where there is God's love in our hearts, there will be a natural reaching out to gather others, giving and showing love. When we are willing to allow God's love to flow through us to others, the blessing is much greater than if we gave out of our own personal storehouses.

Our tendency is to give up too quickly on people who are starved for love. No one is hopeless, and we often give up at the time we most need to persist. Thank God his love keeps on loving and never gives up on us. Paul expressed this in his letter to the Romans, "His kindness and forbearance and patience . . . leads you to repentance" (2:4).

We can take four steps as we learn the constancy of giving love while yearning for a response:

1. Partake of the Love Exchange so that you are experiencing God's love for you. This will make you generous toward others.

2. Ask Jesus for ways to respond more lovingly to others.

3. Learn to look into the spirit of a person and not stop with the flesh (2 Corinthians 5:14-17).

4. Believe God's love will quicken a love response. Lovingly pour out your love to him in prayer, and allow him to work when and how he will.

Divine love is so giving, it never gives up for God's love never fails (1 Corinthians 13:8).

Divine love is willing to suffer long, go through whatever is necessary and never give up, because God's love is committed to us, no matter what we do.

I've long been fascinated and instructed by the efficacious love of Monica, the mother of Augustine. She persistently loved and prayed for him for 35 years. Finally one day he heard the powerful words of God in Romans 13:13-14 and gave himself completely to God.

God's love never fails. Many prayers are yearning to be fulfilled, but we must learn to love continually, not giving up for a moment but believing his love never fails.

Love That Sees What We Can Become

The second quality of God's love is his loving totally and unconditionally yet seeing us as we can become. His

29

love looks beyond the present, and yet we're comfortable with him as we are, because his love is so releasing.

The mother eagle loves the little eaglets as they are in their helplessness, but because she sees them as the mighty eagles they can become, she must stir up the nest. In their early stages of development she may have to spread her wings and catch them, but they will become what they are destined—mighty monarchs of the sky.

When I was 12 years old, I took piano lessons from a man who was a natural-born teacher. He had a marvelous godly gift of seeing one's level of maturity but able also to help you advance toward what you could become.

One late, gloomy November afternoon I was at my piano lesson. Near the end of my lesson, Mr. Meretta suddenly leaned back in his chair, drawing long puffs on his pipe, and announced, "Margaret, I want you to get the Greig A Minor Piano Concerto. You could play that very well."

I was stunned and could only stare at him in unbelief. I could not believe what he had said was for me. None of my other teachers had ever made such a reckless statement as that! It had only been two months since I began studying with him and already he was confident of the vision he had for me.

"You mean the simplified version?"

"No, the real thing, not the simplified version!"

My heart leaped up in my mouth, and in my imagination I heard all the orchestras in the world as they sounded the opening bars of the Greig A Minor Piano Concerto. With this vote of confidence, Mr. Meretta won my heart. He knew every weakness and lazy habit I had, and they were legion, yet he trusted me to master the playing of a great piano work.

My daddy was waiting outside Mr. Meretta's studio in the hallway of the old College of Music building. I could hardly wait to tell him of Mr. Meretta's faith in me. Daddy later said my face was white as a sheet and my eyes like stars.

"Daddy, you'll never guess what Mr. Meretta told me to get! The Greig A Minor Piano Concerto. Not the simplified version!"

"Wonderful, I know you can do it."

What sweet reinforcement of God's love in Mr. Meretta and my father.

I literally floated down two flights of steps to the parking lot, all the while seeing myself brilliantly playing that concerto on the College of Music stage. The ride home was spent talking about how soon we could get the music so I could begin.

My mother was cooking at the stove when I swooped into the kitchen. "Momma, guess what Mr. Meretta told me to get! The Greig A Minor Piano Concerto, not the simplified version!"

Momma was stirring lima beans, and she swung around excitedly to say, "Wonderful, how exciting, I know you can do it!"

Supper that night was a banquet of the finest gourmet foods as far as I was concerned. My piano teacher saw what I could become in the midst of what I was, and my heart was on fire.

I nearly killed myself working on the Greig Concerto, which was not the simplified version! It took two years to get the first movement to recital quality, but in two-and-a-half years I was able to perform the work well. That was a turning point for me, for then my music came alive and I was on my way. Mr. Meretta's confidence in me birthed a feeling of confidence.

Thank God for people who love us into what we can become, people who are not put off by where we are, but love us beyond human love. We can ask ourselves: Who has helped us the most? Hasn't it been people releasing us to be our best, yet totally accepting us as we are?

God's love enables us to become who we are meant to be in him. His love looks beyond the present—its blemishes, its failings, its weaknesses—to what we are destined to become—sons and daughters of the most high God.

Facing ourselves is difficult, but his love enables us to be transformed into his likeness. "For I consider that the sufferings of this present time are not worthy to be compared with the glory that is to be revealed to us" is Paul's way of expressing this in Romans 8:18.

How do we grow in accepting others where they are, yet releasing them to become what they can be in Christ? The following are given as solutions:

1. As we pray for that person, we will begin to see them as Jesus sees them. Act on what you see in prayer, not out of where the person may be now.

2. Prayer will reveal how much God loves that person, and we will become the channels for his love. 1 John 4:11 says, "Beloved, if God so loved us, how we ought to love one another."

3. As we pray for that person, God will flood *us* with love for the person in their process of becoming who they are in him. That love will manifest itself in patience (1 Corinthians 13:4).

4. Divine love is wisdom. We must seek that wisdom in our dealings with others.

5. Participate in the Love Exchange daily.

Writers of the past have spoken of Calvary love which is unselfish transforming love. It becomes our privilege to share in that love as we participate in the Love Exchange.

Correcting and Affirming Love

The third quality of divine love is that it is corrective and affirmative at the same time.

The old mother eagle may have to affirm the babies of her love by carrying them on her pinions. She may also have to correct them by forcing them to try again to fly. Her love for them is so deep she persists in affirmation.

My late twenties and thirties found me straying away from God and his love. Like the mother eagle, God was watching me make the flight attempts in my life. The day he swooped down to catch me lovingly on his great wings was the day my father died. I was alone with my dad in the hospital room. As I watched his frail body turn to clay, I rested on wings of love and returned totally to the Lord on that glorious day.

God had been drawing me back to his nest over the last three years of my father's seven-year struggle with a debilitating disease. During this entire time his faith was such a witness to me. Only the night before he had said, "I am going to fight this thing and be healed." Yes, he was gloriously and totally healed that day. Stepping so peacefully into his heavenly home, he left me with the assurance of God's love for me and all of his creation. My heart was flooded with the love of God.

I did not call the nurse immediately, but allowed a few minutes to seal the surrender and rejoice that Daddy was healed and at home. The assurance came that he was walking and leaping all over heaven. Our family's prayers were gloriously answered.

The nurse stepped into the room and quietly looked around as though sensing the heavenly realm. He saw my peace and joy and asked if I were alright.

"Yes, I'm fine. I've never seen anyone die before. God has healed my dad, and I have come home to God today." My face was radiant and God's presence was real.

"Something has happened, that's for sure," he said. "I'll bring the head nurse."

As he left the room I was flooded with the joyous realization that my dad and I returned home on the same day.

Six o'clock the next morning found me at the high altar of God, which was the old couch in our family room. I was beginning again the journey of prayer. By his grace I would not allow any circumstances to convey the greatest of all lies—that God did not love me or that God would not always stay with me.

The affirmation of God's love that I experienced during those early days 12 years ago was precious. He loved and loved and affirmed and affirmed as only my heavenly Father could. At the same time he was beginning to show me how much I needed to correct some past conduct and attitudes. I needed and wanted to make restitution to all the persons I had hurt. My heart was so loved by him that if I needed to face those unhappy experiences by his grace, I would.

"Lord, let's get going. I believe I can make all the restitution in a few months, don't you?"

"Well, actually, it's going to take about one-and-a-half years to get it all done."

"That long, Lord?"

"Yes, it will take time, but don't fret, only obey every leading I give you."

"I will!"

When we know we are loved God gives such confidence of his love that we can say with the Psalmist, "By Thee I can run upon a troop; And by my God I can leap over a wall" (Psalm 18:29).

In the midst of that restoration process, which indeed did take a year and a half, I was guided one morning in prayer to the powerful passage, "I will not leave you as orphans, I will come to you" (John 14:18).

For years I had been resistant to the Holy Spirit. Numerous people had presented him in ways I could not endorse, and therefore I had shut him out. The fear of losing the strong control I had over my life was threatening, though I was increasingly unhappy and unfulfilled. My musical training and piano practice had been so highly disciplined that a deep rigidity had developed which shut his Spirit completely out. That rigidity became a wall of control that encircled my life, and it manifested itself as resistance to the Spirit, wanting my own way and only accepting him on my terms, according to my theology.

But things were happening in these seven mornings a week, my six to seven o'clock times with God. So thankful to be "back home" with him, I was pouring out my love on him and receiving his love of affirmation in return. While love was flowing between us, God was correcting my attitudes and actions. He constantly revealed my deep needs for restitution and self-knowledge. As this love came to me, I decided that if making things right from my past would aid the intimacy I was experiencing, I was all for it. A flexibility began to emerge every time I humbled myself, confessing my wrongdoing and asking forgiveness. With each time of restitution, more of his love manifested itself and I yearned for all that the Holy Spirit is. I longed to discard this rigid, hard-shell control that I possessed. My prayer life became more and more confessional, allowing his love to be released in me. The more confessional I was of sins and wrongs I had done to others, the more my pride and self-righteousness was broken. This continues

35

to be true today. He was correcting and affirming me all at the same time. How amazing is his tender care!

One lovely morning, during spring break at Asbury College, I went to my place of prayer with such love for Jesus in my heart. For months I had been seeking the Holy Spirit in my life. I was seeking more than just a casual encounter; I wanted the Holy Spirit in my life taking total control.

Over the years I have tried to tell about that glorious morning, but words truly fail. He came that morning as he always comes to those who yearn for him with all their heart. He came with a baptism of holy love, with the fire of the Holy Spirit which burned for four days. The burning was so powerful that first day I had to lie down most of the day. The Holy Spirit came revealing Jesus, and I saw him in my heart as I had never seen him before. I was speechless for I did not want to speak and I couldn't. He taught me and loved me during the duration of the burning. His control during this time was overwhelming, for the Holy Spirit absolutely loved me into total surrender.

This experience continued all day, yet it seemed only a few moments. In the late afternoon I called my mother, who has been my spiritual guide, and sought her counsel. As a wise guide she encouraged me, "Continue to be totally submissive and quiet before him, yielding everything to him."

When my husband stepped through the back door, he sensed God's presence and called out to me, "Are you alright?"

"Oh, John, God has come to me today. It has been incredible! The Holy Spirit has revealed Jesus to me."

The vivid reality of Jesus continued with burning for four days, gently diminishing in its intensity each day. Quietly I stayed in his presence and waited on him while doing little else.

I have never been the same! The afterglow of that encounter with the Trinity lasted one-and-a-half years. One of the results of this eighteen-month experience has been the Love Exchange.

God's love is characterized by such a glorious mixture. For example, as he loves us, he is also leading us into accountability that we could never have faced without his love. That is the message of the twelfth chapter of Hebrews. We have a need for chastening, especially at the present time, but the thought of facing it alone is unbearable. Thank God he loves us enough to correct us with corrective yet affirmative love. One of the surest means of knowing that we belong to God is knowing experientially how he lovingly relates to us in divine affirmation and correction.

The last quality of divine love I consider here is self-forgetfulness.

Self-forgetful Love

The mother eagle's sole focus is on ministering to her children—to aid and guide them until they can mount up with wings and soar into the heavens on their own. What is really happening here? We know the mother eagle wants the eaglets to fly, but the eternal lesson is one of unselfishness. Yes, the mother probably would rather be soaring through the clear spring air unencumbered, but love for her young reigns at this time. The unselfish love God has for us is displayed here between the mother and her fledglings.

As the flow of divine love begins to move in us, we will be enabled more and more to forget about ourselves and be increasingly concerned with God's agenda. Such a change in our attitudes and the direction our life is taking allows for a decreasing amount of self-pity. We see the futility of fretting and stewing and are able to convert those energies into positive growth patterns. Our walk then becomes one where God is allowed to pry loose our total self-preoccupation so our focus is gently but firmly placed on him. With the love the mother eagle has for her offspring there is little or no time for self-preoccupation. Can we say that we have this unselfish love activated in our lives?

Evelyn Underhill has so wisely said, "Real love neutralizes egotism so we worry about ourselves less and we admire and delight in God and his other children more and more. We no longer strive for our own way." This is reminiscent of "If anyone wishes to come after Me, let him deny [or forget about] himself, and take up his cross daily and follow Me" (Luke 9:23).

How do we forget about ourselves?

1. The daily involvement in the Love Exchange is an exercise whereby we concentrate on God for a period of time. Involved in this concentration is to practice self-forgetfulness. For those moments while I receive his love and pour out my love, my attention turns to thinking about his greatness and faithfulness. With my gaze fixed on God I can no longer focus so totally on myself.

2. The Love Exchange slowly but surely begins to release me from any pettiness. By focusing on what sins have been done against me, I keep the focus on me. As the love relationship with God unfolds I begin to get my eyes off my hurts, my pains, and my unforgiveness. Unforgiveness is keeping my eyes on me; while forgiveness, which is probably love's most marvelous empowerment, focuses on what Jesus has done to help me. Calvary love, as the great saints have called it, releases me to forgive and take my eyes off myself, turning my focus on Jesus and all he forgave. Because he forgives,

his love enables me to forgive. As we appreciate Calvary love, we are strengthened to look away from ourselves and onto Jesus.

Parental Love

Hundreds of stories could be told about how God's love has shown through loving mothers and fathers as they minister in self-forgetful ways to their children. My dad used to tell about a father and mother who unselfishly nursed a young son through a terrible sickness during most of his school days. They prayed for and loved this son, forgetting about themselves and allowing God's love to be released. Even the doctors believed it was the unselfish, holy love of God flowing through the parents which saved the young man's life. After entering college it was not long before he turned from God. The chain of events in his life proved too much, and he slipped further and further away.

That father and mother continued to forget about themselves. Though no longer involved in nursing, they were now spending time in intercession. They soon discovered this to be one of the most powerful ways to deny themselves. They entered into a dynamic prayer life, not only for their son but for other children.

They heard nothing from their son for over 20 years. During his absence their love continued. As they prayed, they were more interested in others than themselves. They began to experience a deep knowledge that at the right time and place their son would return to God.

One golden autumn morning the front doorbell rang and there stood their son, willing to give himself to Jesus and be a new creature in Christ. His father and mother were great channels for his homecoming because they laid down their own lives to intercede for him. God answered their prayers.

The question we must be asking is, "Where is my focus?" Still on *me* or is it being gradually shifted so that I gaze on Jesus and outward toward others?

Oh to be cleansed of our self-centeredness so that we look longer and longer at Jesus and less and less at ourselves. Only when we look to him, as in the Love Exchange, is our gaze or focus changed.

How do we begin to allow his divine love to flow through us more and more, loosing us from the shackles of self love?

1. Daily pour out your love on Jesus so that you might receive daily his love for you. Allow the Love Exchange to alter you.

2. Resolve to love as God loves, in all of life's experiences.

3. Look in the Word of God for his glorious words of love for us. This becomes a daily love bath for body, soul and spirit.

4. Act on God's love within you. Listen to the still, small voice within. Even if you are late in obeying, you can begin at any place in a situation.

5. Confess when you fail. Isaiah 48:18 says, "If only you had paid attention to My commandments! Then your well-being would have been like a river, and your righteousness like the waves of the sea."

6. Love never fails. Our trust level or faith level grows as we know God better. Exercise that growing faith as he directs you.

The wonder of all this is that God's love is always moving toward us. If we are obedient to the laws of love, he leads us into higher dimensions of love. If we open ourselves to this divine love, we discover that his love will flow in difficult places. "He made him ride on the high places of the earth . . . and He made him suck honey from the rock, and oil from the flinty rock" (Deuteronomy 32:13).

John Wesley quotes Thomas A. Kempis in *The Christian Pattern*. "He that loves, flies, runs and rejoices, he is free and not bound."

Open to Love

The Love Exchange is like a daily conversation or a daily infilling with the Holy Spirit and his love. This exchange is a way to open ourselves to the love of God and tie it down in a practical way. This book is all about a little pattern, a divine formula, for growing in the love of God.

Paul encouragingly says in Romans 5:5 that "hope does not disappoint, because the love of God has been poured out within our hearts through the Holy Spirit who was given to us." We are born again when this experience comes; we have repented of our sins and are able to receive his love. It is a gift from God, not based on anything within us nor anything we can measure up to or achieve. The rebirth brings with it a whole new concept of loving God, others and self. William Law, in his book *The Power of the Spirit,* developed the following concept: We cannot love God with human love, but rather it is God's love in us that loves God back.

God's love will surge high in new converts. The tragedy is that without nurturing this love it will wane. The implementation of the Love Exchange at this time aids the maturing.

The baptism of the Holy Spirit is a fuller release of divine love, or as I choose to call it, a baptism of divine love. This means that we see more clearly Jesus' nature of love, and we are more under the control of that holy love. "But the Helper, the Holy Spirit, whom the Father will send in My name, He will teach you all things, and bring to your remembrance all that I said to you" (John 14:26). Therefore, he will reveal more of Jesus' love nature and release more of God's love in your life.

I believe that as we yield to the constraint of divine love through the Holy Spirit, Jesus is revealed more and more as the Lord of love. The newly-found lordship of love begins to constrain us to say yes to all the lessons of love. Every entanglement and person in our lives have been authorized by God that we might be victorious in learning to love as he loves us. We begin to see all of life's experiences as ways for learning to love with his love. We soon recognize that the only true mark of Jesus is his free-flowing love in our lives. The mark can never be one of the gifts, nor great spiritual experiences, nor the church to which we belong.

Real growth in love is possible when we say yes to the Lord of love and yes to the lessons of love. He begins to teach us to take seriously the life of prayer, because it is in prayer that God's love is released, and we learn to live with his love.

Only as we partake of his love nature in the Love Exchange does he have the freedom to love through us. We fulfill the royal law of love as mentioned in James 2:8-9, "If, however, you are fulfilling the royal law, according to the Scripture, 'You shall love your neighbor as yourself,' you are doing well. But if you show partiality, you are committing sin and are convicted by the law as transgressors."

Only through the life of prayer can God's love gain more control over us and our love life. We must daily come and drink at the fountain of divine love. Herein lies the purpose of all prayer.

As the prayer closet experience broadens, we discover we are no longer satisfied with this momentary encounter with love. We experience a growing empowerment to practice living in his loving presence all through our daily exchanges. We seek to abide in his love—whether alone with him or in the presence of others.

ॐ•℘

The Love Exchange
is realizing
the deepest need
of the human heart,
which is to love
and be loved
in return.

ॐ•℘

Chapter 3

What Is the Love Exchange?

And he said to him, "'You shall love the Lord your God with all your heart, and with all your soul, and with all your mind.' This is the great and foremost commandment. The second is like it, 'You shall love your neighbor as yourself.' On these two commandments depend the whole Law and the Prophets."

Matthew 22:37-40

The truth of the Love Exchange became apparent to me in 1982. In the months and years since that initial encounter, a series of events all add up to an ever widening experience. After that first Love Exchange that poured out through my spirit, the renewal of my life was so apparent it astonished not only others but myself. The Holy Spirit spoke to me of how this was the life-giving experience of partaking of his divine nature of love. This is also a vital part of our reason and need for prayer. Such prayer is a profound and healing expression of the Godhead, because it brings him close to us, and we are able to appropriate the reality of his love on Calvary.

I was directed to go to the Word of God for instruction and confirmation of these life-giving experiences. Excitement grew as I found one episode after another of people in the New Testament who had given their love to Jesus only to joyously find themselves the recipients of his deep love.

The term *Love Exchange* evolved out of my examination of what had happened to me, coupled with what I saw in Scripture. The definition of this term is threefold with one part flowing naturally into another.

First, the Love Exchange is a realization, a moment of illumination, a reality brought to life in us by the Holy Spirit. When we are open to see who God is, we realize what he means to us and what he has done for us. As a new sense of reality rises up within us we find our love for him defies words. Awkward though it may be, we must speak love to him. Whether it be three minutes or twenty, we take the time to love God, expressing either out loud or within ourselves our love, appreciation, gratitude and thanksgiving to him. Our realization of how we feel about him is basic. Those who know God often experience such joyous love, but they brush it aside and do not take time to get in touch with all the various feelings or stop before full expression has been given.

The first step of the Love Exchange is telling God as freely and totally as we can how much we love him. The ability to do this grows as we grow in loving him. Again, it is important not to brush aside these feelings but rather get in touch with them and freely express them

to Jesus and the Father. The flow of this expression of love will be shockingly brief at first because our love for him is so limited.

A reciprocal rhythm begins as we enter the second aspect of this experience. Now we take time to allow the Holy Spirit to quicken in us the reality that he sheds abroad in us the love of God, as expressed in Romans 5:8. "God demonstrates His own love toward us, in that while we were yet sinners, Christ died for us." As we ponder and meditate on Scriptures that express his love for us, we enter into this love relationship.

Believing and trusting in the Word of God that he really does love me I openly receive that love into my life at that time and place. I appropriate the reality of the Scripture read in my meditation. The Holy Spirit quickens me to believe the Scripture, and in response I raise my hands ceremonially to receive his love for me. We linger in this relationship, of first expressing my love for him, then his love being expressed in the Word of God to me. It is an intimacy which goes beyond anything I can articulate. It is a resting in that love. It is a time of loving and sharing between God and me, expressing by faith that we are one in his love. It is a communion, a fellowship, a renewal time.

The saints in the past have called it contemplation because in this second stage I am more taken up with him. To please God is now the central desire of my prayer rather than thinking of myself. My focus is on God, not myself or my own circumstances. I yearn to be true to him and totally obedient. Our hearts are in communion by faith.

The Love Exchange then is realizing the deepest need of the human heart, which is to love and be loved in return. By the nurturing of our heart and spirit by the heavenly Father, we are nurtured in his love. Paul's prayers are full of growing more and more in his love.

Much literature has been written about contemplation or being self-forgetful, yet absorbed in him. From the vantage point of the Love Exchange, the literature over the centuries has concentrated on our love going out to God with little emphasis on his love coming to us. However, the Bible is full of verses that articulate his love for me. The Love Exchange then is incomplete unless we allow him entry into our lives by faith. To receive his love through allowing the Holy Spirit to quicken love into reality by faith, the truth of the love Scriptures becomes basic to the Love Exchange. This is a biblical approach which appropriates the reality of the love of God for us as stated in the Word.

God speaks love to us through these Scriptures because they contain his words of love. His message has been the same for centuries in the Word of God. Our greatest need is to hear that he truly loves us beyond our wildest dreams. As we slowly and carefully speak these verses aloud we move with the help of the Holy Spirit into the truth and reality of each verse. We believe by faith the validity and reality of the verses and we respond, "Jesus, I believe you love me, you love even me. I open myself to receive your love and receive it by faith."

Many people over the centuries have felt this experience of mutual love was only for those in a cloister, shut off from life and having time for hours of meditation and prayer. However, anyone can spend a few minutes a day loving God and letting him love in return. Do you have three minutes a day to love God and another three minutes to realize his love by faith? Such a love experience is for all Christians everywhere, because it is the core of our walk with Jesus. This relationship must be nurtured and cultivated, and the Love Exchange provides the pathway for us to follow.

Third, as I open my life to receive his divine nature of love and affirming, at a certain time and place I receive his love by faith. This giving and receiving love deepens my capacity to love God and allows his love more permission to transform me into his image. My receptivity and responsiveness to him grows as I lovingly "wait on him," as I love him, allowing him to love me.

Biblical Examples

After any prayer experience with God, I went back to the Bible to see what his Word teaches. To my amazement and for the first time, I recognized the numerous Love Exchanges between Jesus and the people. Many of the old stories took on new meaning in light of my experience.

Probably the most profound example we have is Mary at the tomb, falling at the feet of Jesus in adoration and worship—the highest fulfillment of the Love Exchange as he speaks her name in love and gives his love to her. Out of this magnificent exchange Jesus gives her a charge, a calling to go and tell the others that he is alive. In the Love Exchange, when we are totally forgetful of ourselves, thinking only of God, we receive guidance from him concerning the kingdom and our part in the kingdom. Mary's love was her largest part, but Jesus wants our highest love for him to empower us to go and tell of him. The Love Exchange empowers us for ministry and service (John 20:1-18).

Another example is Mary as she poured out her alabaster box of perfume on Jesus' feet (John 12: 1-8). He received her love and loved her back. So deeply he intended his act of love that no one would forget it. This Love Exchange was a blessing to Jesus at a time of great need. He needs our love and is lonely for our love. As we love him, the Father loves us (John 14:21,23).

It is Mary who chose the better part by sitting at the feet of Jesus and pouring her love out on him. In turn, he sat with her in love. She says nothing, for Jesus was her defense to Martha, a beautiful picture of content-ment, peace, resting and loving (Luke 10:38-42).

It is John who got so close to Jesus that he reclined on his breast. Scripture says of him, "Jesus loved him" (John 13:23).

It is Peter and Jesus on the shore loving one another. After Peter's denial he had a lot to get off his chest so he could once again love Jesus. By that little fire burning with the aroma of broiled fish, Peter was getting every-thing squared away so they could love one another. Only they knew the exchange, but such deep intimacy (John 21:1-17)!

It is the prodigal son being met on the road by his father running to meet him with a loving embrace. As he made the first step of love, his father ran to return that love. As we love God, he will break in on us, and we will know his love before we are finished. As we draw near to him, he draws near to us (Luke 15:11-24).

It could have been the rich young ruler. Jesus gave his love, but it was not reciprocated. The Love Exchange was aborted (Matthew 19:16-22).

Today's Example

Should such encounters seem impossible for us today, here is another contemporary example for our en-couragement.

A lovely young mother, harassed and busy working outside the home, was sitting in her 20-minute prayer time before dashing off to work. It had always been difficult for her to believe God really cared about her or even knew who she was or where she lived. But for eight or nine months she had been setting aside 20 minutes a day for Bible reading and prayer. Though she did not have much love for God, she had been taking several minutes a day to tell him she appreciated him, seeking to express her gratitude.

She had continued this for weeks, and on this particular morning she felt more enthusiasm for telling God she loved him than she had experienced before. She was repeating aloud the tender verses of Isaiah 43:2, "When you pass through the waters, I will be with you; and through the rivers, they will not overflow you. When you walk through the fire, you will not be scorched." These words of love from God were quickened by the Holy Spirit and God revealed himself as her father, her Daddy who loved her. Her tears began to flow as a deep sense of his love for her came down over her. His love became a reality to her.

As she shared this wonderful experience a few days later, tears of joy, "liquid joy" as my mother calls it, flowed down her face. This was her first real experience of knowing God truly loved her, and she had been seeking to follow him for years. As she loved him, God revealed to her his deep love and it poured through her spirit and her soul. She knew him as Daddy, and she knew she was his loved child.

How do we find ourselves in a position to experience the Love Exchange? We have all been told we should do certain things in our lives but with little or no instruction as to how. To say to seek this Love Exchange relationship and not explain how would simply be another frustrating directive. I will lay out a pattern I have experienced in an attempt to make it possible for you.

Many psychologists are saying today that couples should hold one another for at least ten minutes each day, saying very little, but simply letting love flow back and forth between husband and wife. This becomes a time of comforting by being close to one's mate, a time of reinforcing the relationship by being totally present with one another in loving touch. So too, if we are to be involved in a love relationship with God, we need time to embrace his Spirit, and let him embrace our spirit.

Begin now the spiritual exercise of the Love Exchange:

1. Find a quiet place, a regular time, and sit in a relaxed way so you might love God and allow him to love you.

2. Allow this Love Exchange to come at the end of your Bible reading or at the beginning of your time alone with God.

3. Ask the Holy Spirit to help you give and receive love.

4. Get in touch with all or any feelings of love, goodwill, appreciation or gratitude you have for God and begin to speak these affections aloud to him so you can hear them. Such feelings may only be momentary, but continue as long as possible to express your feelings to him.

When we first begin this spiritual exercise it is shocking to see how little we love him. How passive we are, particularly if God has not performed some deed we feel he should perform. We find loving him difficult when he is not busying himself for us and our demands. However, a daily speaking forth of our love for him causes our love for him to increase. As our love for him increases we experience more love coming from him. We can say with John, "We love, because he first loved us" (I John 4:19). Most of our earliest feelings of love and probably some of our deepest expressions of love are those of thanksgiving.

At the outset allow yourself to feel as deeply as you can, for as long as you can even if it is only three minutes a day. Once the final offering of love has been uttered, the focus changes.

5. Give God opportunity to love you—set aside the equal amount of time you have been loving him. Now the most important part of this exchange, his response to you, is experienced.

This whole process of receiving his love begins as such truths as, "God, you love me, you . . . love . . . me," are repeated slowly and prayerfully. Have available a love verse that affirms his love for you. Continue to repeat one or two such verses slowly and thoughtfully so you can hear the truth as it comes from him to minister to you. The following Scriptures are some of the great love texts to be repeated.

Love Passages

Psalm 139:17-18

> How precious also are Thy thoughts to me, oh God!
> How vast is the sum of them!

If I should count them, they would out-
number the sand.
When I awake, I am still with Thee.

Proverbs 8:17

I love those who love me;
And those who diligently seek me will
find me.

Song of Solomon 1:15

How beautiful you are, my darling,
How beautiful you are!
Your eyes are like doves.

Song of Solomon 2:10

My beloved responded and said to me,
"Arise, my darling, my beautiful one,
And come along."

Song of Solomon 2:14

O my dove, in the clefts of the rock,
In the secret place of the steep pathway,
Let me see your form,
Let me hear your voice,
For your voice is sweet,
And your form is lovely.

Song of Solomon 4:7

You are altogether beautiful, my darling,
And there is no blemish in you.

Isaiah 30:18

> Therefore the Lord longs to be gracious to you,
> And therefore He waits on high to have compassion on you.
> For the Lord is a God of justice;
> How blessed are all those who long for Him.

Isaiah 38:17

> Lo, for my own welfare I had great bitterness;
> It is Thou who hast kept my soul from the pit of nothingness,
> For Thou hast cast all my sins behind Thy back.

Isaiah 41:9

> You whom I have taken from the ends of the earth,
> And called from its remotest parts,
> And said to you, "You are My servant,
> I have chosen you and not rejected you."

Isaiah 41:18

> I will open rivers on the bare heights,
> And springs in the midst of the valleys;
> I will make the wilderness a pool of water,
> And the dry land fountains of water.

Isaiah 43:1-2, 4, 25

But now, thus says the Lord, your Creator,
O Jacob,
And He who formed you, O Israel,
"Do not fear, for I have redeemed you;
I have called you by name; you are Mine!

"When you pass through the waters, I will
be with you;
And through the rivers, they will not
overflow you.
When you walk through the fire, you will
not be scorched,
Nor will the flame burn you.

"Since you are precious in My sight,
Since you are honored and I love you,
I will give other men in your place and
other peoples in exchange for your life.

"I, even I, am the one who wipes out your
transgressions for My own sake;
And I will not remember your sins."

Isaiah 44:3-4

For I will pour out water on the thirsty
land
And streams on the dry ground;
I will pour out My spirit on your offspring,
And My blessing on your descendants;

And they will spring up among the grass
Like poplars by streams of water.

Isaiah 45:2-3

> I will go before you and make the rough
> places smooth;
> I will shatter the doors of bronze, and cut
> through their iron bars.
>
> And I will give you the treasures of dark-
> ness
> And hidden wealth of secret places,
> In order that you may know that it is I,
> The Lord, the God of Israel, who calls you
> by your name.

Isaiah 46:4

> "Even to your old age, I shall be the same,
> And even to your graying years I shall
> bear you!
> I have done it, and I shall carry you;
> And I shall bear you, and I shall deliver
> you.

Isaiah 49:15-16

> Can a woman forget her nursing child,
> And have no compassion on the son of
> her womb?
> Even these may forget, but I will not for-
> get you.
>
> Behold, I have inscribed you on the palms
> of My hands;
> Your walls are continually before Me.

Isaiah 51:3, 11-12a

> Indeed, the Lord will comfort Zion;
> He will comfort all her waste places.
> And her wilderness He will make like Eden,
> And her desert like the garden of the Lord;
> Joy and gladness will be found in her,
> Thanksgiving and sound of a melody.
>
> So the ransomed of the Lord will return,
> And come with joyful shouting to Zion;
> And everlasting joy will be on their heads.
> They will obtain gladness and joy,
> And sorrow and sighing will flee away.
>
> I, even I, am He who comforts you.
> Who are you that you are afraid of man who dies.

Isaiah 54:5, 10, 17

> "For your husband is your Maker,
> Whose name is the Lord of hosts;
> And your Redeemer is the Holy One of Israel,
> Who is called the God of all the earth.
>
> "For the mountains may be removed and the hills may shake,
> But My lovingkindness will not be removed from you,

And My covenant of peace will not be
shaken,"
Says the Lord who has compassion on you.

"No weapon that is formed against you
shall prosper;
And every tongue that accuses you in
judgment you will condemn.
This is the heritage of the servants of the
Lord,
And their vindication is from Me,"
declares the Lord.

Isaiah 61:3, 10

To grant those who mourn in Zion,
Giving them a garland instead of ashes,
The oil of gladness instead of mourning,
The mantle of praise instead of a spirit of
fainting.
So they will be called oaks of righteous-
ness,
The planting of the Lord, that He may be
glorified.
I will rejoice greatly in the Lord, My soul
will exult in my God;
For He has clothed me with garments of
salvation,
He has wrapped me with a robe of
righteousness,

As a bridegroom decks himself with a garland,
And as a bride adorns herself with her
jewels.

Isaiah 63:9

In all their affliction He was afflicted,
And the angel of His presence saved them;
In His love and in His mercy He
redeemed them;
And He lifted them and carried them all
the days of old.

Isaiah 66:12-13

For thus says the Lord, "Behold, I extend
peace to her like a river,
And the glory of the nations like an overflowing stream;
And you shall be nursed, you shall be carried on the hip and fondled on the knees.

"As one whom his mother comforts, so I
will comfort you;
and you shall be comforted in Jerusalem."

Jeremiah 31:3

The Lord appeared to him from afar,
saying,
"I have loved you with an everlasting love;
Therefore I have drawn you with
lovingkindness."

Hosea 2:19

> And I will betroth you to Me forever;
> Yes, I will betroth you to Me in righteous-
> ness and in justice,
> In lovingkindness and in compassion.

Zephaniah 3:17

> The Lord your God is in your midst,
> A victorious warrior.
> He will exult over you with joy,
> He will be quiet in His love,
> He will rejoice over you with shouts of joy.

John 3:16

> For God so loved the world, that He gave
> his only begotten Son, that whoever
> believes in Him should not perish, but have
> eternal life.

John 14: 21, 23

> "He who has My commandments and
> keeps them, he it is who loves Me; and he
> who loves Me shall be loved by My Father,
> and I will love him, and will disclose Myself
> to him." Jesus answered and said to him, "If
> anyone loves Me, he will keep My word; and
> My Father will love him, and We will come
> to him, and make Our abode with him."

John 15:9

Just as the Father has loved Me, I have also loved you; abide in My love.

John 16:27

For the Father Himself loves you, because you have loved Me, and have believed that I came forth from the Father.

John 17:23

I in them, and Thou in Me, that they may be perfected in unity, that the world may know that Thou didst send Me, and didst love them, even as Thou didst love Me.

Romans 5:8

But God demonstrates His own love toward us, in that while we were yet sinners, Christ died for us.

Romans 8:37

But in all these things we overwhelmingly conquer through Him who loved us.

1 Corinthians 8:3

> If anyone loves God, he is known by Him.

Galatians 2:20

> I have been crucified with Christ; and it is no longer I who live, but Christ lives in me; and the life which I now live in the flesh I live by faith in the Son of God, who loved me, and delivered Himself up for me."

Ephesians 1:5-6

> He predestined us to adoption as sons through Jesus Christ to Himself, according to the kind intention of His will, to the praise of the glory of His grace, which He freely bestowed on us in the Beloved.

Ephesians 2:4-7

> But God, being rich in mercy, because of His great love with which He loved us, even when we were dead in our transgressions, made us alive together with Christ (by grace you have been saved), and raised us up with Him, and seated us with Him in the heavenly places, in Christ Jesus, in order that in the ages to come He might show the surpassing riches of His grace in kindness toward us in Christ Jesus.

Colossians 1:27

> to whom God willed to make known what is the riches of the glory of this mystery among the Gentiles, which is Christ in you, the hope of glory.

2 Peter 1:3-4

> seeing that His divine power has granted to us everything pertaining to life and godliness, through the true knowledge of Him who called us by His own glory and excellence. For by these He has granted to us His precious and magnificent promises, in order that by them you might become partakers of the divine nature, having escaped the corruption that is in the world by lust.

1 John 3:1-2

> See how great a love the Father has bestowed upon us, that we should be called children of God; and such we are. For this reason the world does not know us, because it did not know Him.
>
> Beloved, now we are children of God, and it has not appeared as yet what we shall be. We know that, when He appears, we shall be like Him, because we shall see Him just as He is.

1 John 4:16, 19

> And we have come to know and have
> believed the love which God has for us. God
> is love, and the one who abides in love
> abides in God, and God abides in him. We
> love, because He first loved us.

Revelation 1:5-6

> and from Jesus Christ, the faithful witness,
> the first-born of the dead, and the ruler of
> the kings of the earth. To Him who loves
> us, and released us from our sins by His
> blood. And He has made us to be a
> kingdom, priests to His God and Father;
> to Him be the glory and the dominion
> forever and ever. Amen.

6. Lift up your arms to him and say, "Lord, I receive your love now, by faith I receive your love. Thank you, God." While our mental response is in the repetition and pondering of Scripture, our physical response might be outstretched hands as commended in Scripture.

7. Believe by faith that you have received God's love, allowing several minutes to rest in his love for you and yours for him. Do not be discouraged if there seems to be no emotional response. This Love Exchange is a transaction by faith, so receive it by faith. The Christian walks by faith, therefore receive his love by faith as a part of this walk. Receive it regardless of what you may experience at the feeling level.

The development of this Love Exchange will result in an intermingling of our love and his love. Often before I finish my part, God leaps in and affirms how much he loves me. I become more open and receptive to his many movements of love to me. Sometimes he gives me the strong message of how much he cares for me, when my response to him has been pitifully weak. I know I am loved. He will multiply our love for him as we practice the Love Exchange

Respond in Faith

In our world today where our emotions are central to much of our experiential life, it becomes our understanding that emotional responses should be a part of our prayer life as well. Let me clarify that this is a faith venture. Our response to God and his response to us is in faith. If we experience no great warm feelings, it does not mean that he has absented himself from us for he will never forsake his commitment to us. Should he quicken our emotions, it is his prerogative. Because he is a God of love, love is always flowing out to us, but the amount of love we receive is determined by our ability to receive. This ability to love and be loved is deepened as we practice and participate in the Love Exchange.

The following two stories illustrate the Love Exchange as it has manifested itself in the lives of people just like you and me.

A young professional woman I know had always felt God was stern and far removed from her. She said she always pictured God high on a throne, and she could see herself standing at the foot of a long stairs leading up to his throne. He never asked for her to come any closer. Inside her was an urge to run up those steps and jump on his lap, but she felt afraid even to ask him if it were possible to ascend the stairs. All of these years she remained at the bottom, far away from God but in his presence.

After some months in the Love Exchange, God leaned out over his chair one day and asked her to come closer. She came up the stairs and arrived at his platform. He reached out his hand and drew her close. She leaned against his chest as he drew her close to his heart. She was able to tell him how much he meant, and he poured out his love on her.

As she told me about this loving episode, she was full of joy. The distance between God and this dear young woman existed no longer. The Love Exchange brought her close to him, and with the marvel of this discovery she knew he truly cared for her.

A young man was seeking to give God ten to fifteen minutes each day. In the pattern of the Love Exchange he spent at least three or four minutes pouring out all the love he could muster on God and waiting three to four minutes to meditate and to receive by faith God's love for him. He had been doing this several months and he felt much better about himself. His sense of personal worth was higher than it had ever been.

One Sunday morning in church, when the pastor invited people to come forward during the pastoral prayer to kneel at the altar to pray, he went forward. This young man knelt to pray and tell God how much he loved him. Suddenly there swept over him the almost blinding sense of God's love for him. He fought for control; he hardly wanted to burst into tears in front of the whole congregation, but he had never before been so deeply aware of God's love, touching his mind, spirit and soul with such unmistakable power. For several minutes he could not get up had he wanted to. He was glad for a long pastoral prayer that morning! When he left the altar he left a new person. He knew he was loved by God as he had never known it before.

There seems to be a super love strategy going around these days. God is eager to manifest himself as friend, Redeemer, Savior and lover of our souls. He is coming to his children by faith and flooding all our lives as he did in these cases. One thing for sure, he wants us to know by his words of love in the Bible and his presence through the Holy Spirit, that he truly is love and loves us with an undying eternal love.

The Love Exchange is a pattern in which we move into the reality of the love verses. As we linger in a focused way on those statements of God, we set the stage for him to manifest himself to us. We begin by loving him in the most energetic way we can, and then by faith know he means what he says in the words of love contained in Scripture. These moments allow God time to reveal the truth of his everlasting love for us through the Holy Spirit.

Exercise. Enter into the Love Exchange as outlined above. A helpful means of speaking the truth of his love for us is to sing of this truth. The following song has been meaningful for many. It is a perfect Love Exchange. It may be helpful to you.

> Lord, You are more precious than silver.
> Lord, You are more costly than gold.
> Lord, You are more beautiful than diamonds

And nothing I desire compares with
  you.

As you sing this song in your devotional time, you can practice the Love Exchange by substituting the word "child" for "Lord." As you sing, imagine him singing it back to you.

ဢ•ဢ

The Love Exchange
brings about a tremendous
impetus to our prayer life,
because we call on him
more out of understanding
his love nature
and goodness.

ဢ•ဢ

Chapter 4

Benefits of the Love Exchange

Because he has loved Me, therefore I will deliver him;
I will set him securely on high, because he has known My name.
He will call upon Me and I will answer him;
I will be with him in trouble;
I will rescue him, and honor him.
With a long life I will satisfy him,
And let him behold My salvation."

Psalm 91:14-16

In these three verses we find in capsule form the results of the Love Exchange. How else can we grow in the depth of God's love if we do not participate actively to exercise the love we have for him? He seems to be bending over backwards to release his love in me in the ways mentioned in Psalm 91. What beautiful promises his love gives to us, and only his love can reveal and provide these. As the revelation takes place, God unfolds more of himself, and we love him more. He always loves more and gives more than is ever possible for us to do. He enjoys revealing what his love is like and pouring out on us all we need in him.

Though it has been some years ago since I started the Love Exchange, I can distinctly remember the unbelievable thrill when God began to reveal the truth that he truly loved me. That was then and is currently my most poignant need—to believe and know in my deepest self that God loves me and will always love me.

I remember my first response to God as being one of caution, uncertainty and fear as I began meeting with him at six o'clock every morning. I knew to some degree that he loved me, but I was coming from years of being backslidden from God. Might he not discipline me fairly severely? Did he still love me as before? Was he really there for me, as in the old days? What was his love nature like? I had prayed constantly during my backslidden days, "Oh, Lord, don't give up on me, don't leave me. I am coming back to you someday." But now that I was back, what could I expect?

Experientially I did not believe God loved me. In my head I knew he loved me, but in my heart it remained to be seen. How deep did the love go? My spirit needed to experience his love, day after day, week after week, to know his unconditional love. I had experienced his love thousands of times in the past, before turning away from him. But I had been so unfaithful for so many years!

To believe experientially that he did truly love me was difficult. I knew he loved others. But me? The longer I had gone against God the more fear I had that he was fed up with me. So the daily Love Exchange was entered into with some nervousness and trepidation.

The basic benefit of the Love Exchange is expressed in Psalm 91:14, " . . . I will deliver him." I believe the deliverance is from the fear that God does not and could not love us as we are.

God Loves You and Me

The Love Exchange was one way I could begin the lifetime journey of having my deepest need met. That need was to believe that God loves me, just as I am with no strings attached. Day after day, week after week, I came giving God such limited love as I had. To my utter amazement the words of love from Scriptures, on which I had been meditating, continued to reiterate the same thing. The message clearly cried, "I love you, I love you, I love you, Margaret. There is nothing you can do that keeps me from loving you. I love you with an everlasting love." Could it be true? Were these words true? In faith, as I said, "Lord, I receive your love for me," something was happening to me. I began to believe it on an ever-deepening plane of consciousness. As it began to penetrate down to my real self, I found myself living out of the truth that he loved who I really was.

A precious reality began to steal over me during my normal work day. In the midst of busyness and activity a still small voice would whisper deep in my heart, "I love you, Margaret."

"Oh, Lord, I love you too. You are precious to me, Lord. You are everything to me."

"Relax now in my love," came his continuing assurance.

"Lord, I am trying, it's so exciting."

Love began to spill into my inner life, not only in the Love Exchange but also during the day. Deep inside my spirit I began to accept the truth of his words of love from the hour of prayer. My sense of well-being was embraced as God loved me, a sense of rightness within resulting from experiencing God loving me daily. It made me feel good about myself, for God really cared for me and reassured me so many times during the day.

God and I were having little Love Exchanges going to work, at work, leaving work, at home, all the time, even when I failed and failed badly, many, many times. When I would get up and run back to God, he always greeted me with open arms of love. It is a joyful discovery each time we fail to find him unchanged in his attitude toward us. How that humbles us and causes us to love him more and more. My concept of how much he loves me developed more from my failures of living in that love than nearly any other way except the Love Exchange itself. My failures allowed him to prove over and over the awesome fact—*I love you!*

Six months into this wondrous discovery of God's love for me, a student stopped me in the hall at Asbury College where I was teaching at the time.

"Mrs. Therkelsen, there is something going on with you. You look different somehow, softer. What is going on?"

I grabbed that young girl and gave her a big hug. "I'm so glad you can see something happening. I know a secret!" I was beaming from ear to ear as we spoke.

Her eyes were wide, "What is it?"

"I am discovering how much God really and truly loves me." Looking at her, I continued, "And how he loves you!"

Big tears filled her eyes and with another quick hug she said, "Thanks, Mrs. T., I really needed to hear that today. I'll say one thing, if you can change like this, I want what you have!"

The first benefit of the Love Exchange is the discovery that God loves you and me. Isn't his love glorious! This is the basic benefit, the most needed reality in your life and mine, that he truly loves us and always will. To experience this love in a growing friendship every moment of every day is life's highest experience.

Satan's Lies

As we experience his love in the Love Exchange a second benefit begins to emerge—that God sets us above the lie of Satan that says God is not a good God. There are two great lies perpetuated by Satan. One is that God does not care anything about me because I am too bad. Second, God is not worth loving because you cannot believe he is good. We are set above these lies because we know his nature of love and goodness from our involvement in the Love Exchange.

I don't know of any areas with more disbelief than (1) God loves me and (2) God is a good God. The major issue that took me off my spiritual track for over 13 years, beginning in my twenties, was just this fact. My concept of God was that he was not totally good; his ways not just; and that he was not a God of faithfulness. He was not as Moses proclaimed him: "The Rock! His work is perfect, for all his ways are just; a God of faithfulness and without injustice, righteous and upright is He" (Deuteronomy 32:4).

I did not understand many things in those early years. Being young and rebellious, my self-willed nature did not know the extent of our world's sinfulness and failures, nor understand Satan's constant ploys to cause us to believe that our heavenly Father's character is questionable. Satan's greatest activity among Christians is to malign our heavenly Father's character any way he can. How can God be good and allow this or that to happen? How can he be trusted? Is he a God of love if he lets such and such come about?

The Love Exchange began to develop a willingness on my part, empowered by the growing truth that God truly loved me, to allow him to teach me that he was and is good! What had happened to me in believing the most awful lie of Satan, that God was not trustworthy and not faithful, was that I abandoned him and blamed him for things that were not his fault. Now his love was making me more open and more responsive, allowing him to teach me the truth as he loved me. Through the Love Exchange, as his love ministered to all my wounds, came the joyous song that this glorious love is pure and redemptive because he is totally and completely good. God revealed how I had allowed my blaming nature to push onto him what was my fault and my choice, also how I had moved out of his love as I saw others, whom I had trusted, betray Jesus by not being honest and fair.

What a revelation comes when we allow God to love us! He begins to show us how the consequences of our choices have caused certain things to happen, choices we have made out of our own self-will which he allows to be fulfilled. We take matters into our own hands and then blame him. As he showed me the whys and wherefores of my past, I began to see that God is good! What relief, what joy! But best of all, I was willing, by his grace, to face my decisions which shut him out.

Over these last eight years I have come to know experientially two of God's deepest truths—that he loves me and that he is all good. There is no shadow of turning in him who is utterly and totally dependable. His goodness will stand for all eternity, and I can rest in it. No matter what may or may not happen to me and mine, God is love and he is good. To know this in our spirits releases eternal joy, and that joy becomes real as we linger in his presence, receiving his love and his goodness.

I knew from my head to my feet, inside and outside, that "Thou art good and doest good" as Psalm 119:68 claims. It's been a long journey to believe him completely, but it is only as I know God in the Love Exchange that he keeps on showering me with his divine love, no matter what I am or say. This perfect love proves to me his total goodness.

Eternal Goodness, Growing Faith

What is the result of experientially knowing that God loves me and he is good? An inevitable confidence and faith in him. The more we know him, the more we love him and the more we trust him. This then becomes the third benefit. It follows that we can relax in his love and goodness and trust his love and goodness. As the Love Exchange progresses, our faith in him grows. We know more sides of his personality and character. It is in the loving where we learn to trust him as "faith working through love" (Galatians 5:6).

All the years I was away from God I had a deep uneasiness and fear. Heaviness and sadness spoiled happy experiences, for I had turned my back on the truth of God loving me. My trust level was so low I could not trust myself or others. Only by appropriating his love in the Love Exchange did God bring me back to trust him.

Answered Prayer

The fourth benefit is that when we call on God we know he will answer. The Love Exchange brings about a tremendous impetus to our prayer life, because we call on him more out of understanding his love nature and goodness. Thus my prayers are closer to his heart and will. When God sees us seeking to love him and obey his love commandments, he answers us. He responds because his love must express itself. Prayer is a dialogue, an exchange of love whereby we are moving more on his wavelength and the potentialities of his responding.

God Is With Me

As I experience personal challenges and trouble, his presence is made real to me. I know I am not alone. Everything will be and is well because God is with me. As Psalm 23 says, "He is my shepherd and is leading me, spreading a table in the midst of my enemies, and I want for nothing because he is near". This fifth benefit: we are assured of his presence in times of trouble.

The depth of this was tested several years into the Love Exchange when we discovered a serious arthritic condition in my back, and my future health did not look good. My doctor was deeply concerned about the pain I was experiencing, and the prospects of living normally and without medication were minimal.

Following a prayer service for healing where my need was lifted along with several others, I believe God spoke to me about trusting his love for healing. Indeed I was healed, but I had to trust him over a period of time. His pattern was laid out by him and I was to obey. I lived with severe pain for four months, but I knew I was whole, and indeed I was and I am. Eight years later I have no pain in my back today due to his healing love.

God hears when we call on him, and he is with us in trouble. We realize his presence in the Love Exchange, and we carry this into any and all problems and troubles we may experience. Whatever the outcome, he is with us! Such comfort and grace is available for us. Tremendous multiplication of his love comes when his children face problems.

Rescuing Love

The sixth benefit is "I will rescue him and honor him" (Psalm 91:15). I believe the Love Exchange begins to rescue us from ourselves when we recognize God's favor or blessing present in our lives. We need to be rescued from ourselves and our past that we may know experientially his favor or love blessings on us.

We innocently think that all we experience is what we perceive consciously, but deep below the surface of the conscious mind God is dealing with many concerns. He has a huge job to do in our emotional life and in our human spirit. It is a lifetime process of being changed into his likeness. We need rescuing from many of our old emotional patterns and from refusing the self-knowledge he wants us to have. In order to be rescued we must face ourselves, and in the process his love will rescue us and lift us up from being lost in our failures and mistakes. God wants a wholeness in our emotional and thought life, and he wants our wills to be more and more in touch with his will and obedient to it. His desire is to have who we are in him to be the seat of our living. Then our human spirit is able to respond to the Holy Spirit within.

The power of the Love Exchange is in the constant reassurance that God cares, and as we draw ever nearer to him we learn he can bring up in us the courage to face whatever comes our way. With him we face the woundedness in our emotional life and the rebellion and self-will in our spiritual life. What a magnificent, skilled architect the heavenly Father is! He loves us so much that he brings our whole inner and outer life into harmony with his highest good for us. This inward unity of soul and spirit is our only real bulwark against loneliness. We will feel lonely as long as we are so broken within that we can't fellowship with God.

Among my acquaintances is a woman so wounded by her past she had little self-esteem when I met her. But in her brokenness she was as open as she could be to God's will. Her father's continual rejection of her left her without the sense of worth and approval necessary to feel good about herself. Over a period of three years she had been practicing the Love Exchange as a part of her quiet time. She also had often interaction in a counseling setting during that period. Though painful at first, she opened herself up to others and most of all to God and his love.

Her involvement with the Love Exchange was not a daily experience, but she did enter into that relationship several times a week. At the end of the three-year period, she was experiencing self-worth but had received God's love only by faith in the exchange.

One morning she was having her quiet time, and crying out to God, when suddenly she saw herself leaning against God himself. She felt an arm steal lovingly around her, and she sensed his deep love for her. She nestled close to him and simply relaxed. Crying her heart out over the rejection she had felt from her father, so common in our society today, she heard God speak to her about his everlasting love for her and how precious she was to him. She wept like a baby as he "fathered" her in beautiful love. Something happened in her emotional life that day. The very point where she had felt rejected by her earthly father and made to feel worthless, she now felt accepted and totally loved by her heavenly Daddy. She felt herself worth the price of Jesus suffering on the cross. God's love burst in on her emotional and spiritual awareness, and she was changed into a person not rejected but loved by God Almighty.

What a profound experience this was on her life, and she has not been the same since. She still has a long distance to go, but she is on her journey. God integrated in his love her emotional and spiritual life. She has received his blessing and favor as she has allowed him to rescue her from herself. Her emotional wounds of rejection were healed as she let him be her Daddy that day.

"With a long life I will satisfy him, and let him behold My salvation" (Psalm 91:16). The seventh benefit to come out of the Love Exchange is that we begin to move into God's place for us in the kingdom of God. God's eternal place for us, his divine place, begins to come forth.

As I linger in Jesus' presence, loving him with increasing love and becoming more freed up to receive his love, a deep sense of contentment and peace wells up within me. He is opening doors for what he wants me to do in his kingdom. I begin to see his opening up the process of working out my salvation, and the eternal will of God begins to unfold inside of me. All of this comes while all I am doing is loving him and being receptive to his love. Everything else flows out of that glorious love experience.

The gifts God has given me begin to push out like the small green leaves of a bush in early spring (Proverbs 18:16). They are little promises that are complete in themselves, for as they mature they become an enlarged version of the beginning promise. During all this I am only seeking to be faithful in love. He will take care of opening and shutting the proper doors. As we are obedient in small things, he opens up a pathway to walk on. Do not minimize, however, what is involved in obeying the love commandments.

Lay It Down

About five years ago, as I was resting in the love of God, I heard him speak to me, "I want you to leave the music field, lay it down completely and move out into the area of prayer as your vocation. As a move in that direction, I want you in school getting a degree in marital and family counseling so you can be better equipped to help others by understanding human nature."

The curious thing about that guidance was I had heard God speak this same message to my emotions and spirit on different occasions several years before. Following a recital or performance I would hear a fleeting but powerful message as wind plays on a wind chime, "It's over, I need you in another place. It's done, lay it down."

For years my whole life had been wrapped around music and its discipline. Now as the Love Exchange deepened over the years, I had a sense of my life being broadened, reaching out in different directions, yearning for a deeper fulfillment. My inward desire was to be in the ultimate place God wanted me, where he would flow through me in the fullest way. My ministry in music had been a joy, but my soul and spirit were now being drawn in a way I knew not and yet a way that seemed most comfortable and familiar. All of this developed as I went quietly about my business and enjoyed loving God and letting him love me.

Such a sense of contentment is based on the sure knowledge that all is well and that it is his job to guide me. In the exchange I often had an awareness of excitement on his part when I relinquished everything to him and said, "Yes, Lord, you gave me the music and you can surely take it away. It's yours. I don't have anything but what you've given me."

He rescues us from lesser places and lesser concerns to move us into his perfect place for us here. He needs us where we can be of the most benefit to him and where he can flow through us in more unhindered ways.

God lets us behold his salvation coming in the various settings where he places us. He moves us into our life work as we love him and let him love us. He is the initiator; we merely follow him as he opens the doors.

These benefits and others are the reality and consequences of allowing God to fulfill his covenant word to us. He has promised to care for us and be all in all to us. The covenant that exists between God and his people depends on realizing my part of the covenant. Participating in his great plan is possible only as I obey what he has told me. He is able surely and certainly to do his part. It is through my obedience to his love commands that wholeness comes in body, soul and spirit.

꧁ • ꧂

I realize some people
are so damaged
they can barely sit
in God's presence.
But if they are willing to go
with Jesus on this journey,
there can be help
for them.

꧁ • ꧂

Chapter 5

Barriers to the Love Exchange

Blessed be the Lord,
For He has made marvelous
His lovingkindness to me in a besieged city.
As for me, I said in my alarm,
"I am cut off from before Thine eyes";
Nevertheless Thou didst hear the voice of my
supplications
When I cried to Thee."

Psalm 31:21-22

Ken was a strong, athletic young man who had discovered the joy of spending some time each morning with God. He had been reared in the church, and his family was active in all the functions of church life. According to head knowledge Ken sensed that God loved him. In his heart, however, he did not have the assurance that this was true. But how he wanted it to be so!

Caught up in sports, college, first job and a real love for people, he was giving less and less time to God. It dawned on him one evening, as he ran from one committment to another, that he was doing exactly what his dad had always done. He never had much time for Ken nor his two sisters—too busy helping everyone else. *I'm doing the same thing running here and there*, Ken thought, *I have no time for God or myself.*

In my first conversation with him I suggested the Love Exchange. Experimenting with the pattern seemed to intrigue him, so he agreed to fifteen minutes each morning, six or seven minutes of that time to be spent in the Love Exchange.

A few months later, during one of those early morning hours, God broke in on Ken and affirmed the love verse, "I have loved you with an everlasting love" (Jeremiah 31:3). There arose from within him a heart cry, "Lord, you have always been too busy for me, just like my dad was too busy for me. I cannot believe you really love me. I have never seen you show that love and I cannot receive your love, not even by faith."

Ken's response was quite revealing. As we talked about this interaction with God, he was able to see that he had transferred to his image of God the alienation he'd felt toward his father, who had been so consumed with other things in life there had been no time for his son.

Often we erect barriers to receiving God's love by faith—as seen in the example of Ken. He soon found himself in a spiritually-directed counseling setting and began to face his hurt caused by the rejection of his father. He continued the daily interaction with God in the Love Exchange as a spiritual exercise during those days of counseling. Today, three years later, Ken is able to know and believe God does indeed love him. No

longer does the limited love image received from his father permeate his concept of God's love for him.

Perhaps this story has brought to mind other examples of barriers. What are some barriers that prevent us from being able to believe that God loves us?

Inability to Receive Love

Probably the most common barrier and the one presenting the greatest difficulty to rise above is the problem of not being able to receive love. If our earthly fathers did not give us love as children, today we lack the ability to receive love from anyone, especially God. Perhaps our earthly fathers were physically absent, or though physically present they were emotionally distanced, making it in either case impossible for any male nurturing to transpire. Many people had fathers in their homes during childhood, but their demeanor was so stern and nonexpressive of feelings of love for their children, that no love was expressed either in verbal or physical articulation. When there is no verbal or physical warmth shown during those formative years we tend to feel God must love in the same way. God may be there, but he is non-accepting and non-expressive in his love. The emotional absence of a father is devastating to any child for many reasons, not the least of which is that his concept of God comes from the father's ability to relate and meet his nurturing needs.

Either the emotional or physical absence of the father is profoundly reflected in how one perceives God. Should our earthly fathers be approachable—allowing us to speak out of our feelings—and they accept us in love, then these qualities are transfered to God. The degree of ease to which the Love Exchange is practiced will be determined at the outset by the love we have known from our physical fathers. Challenges will always exist, however, as none of us has been nurtured as completely as our heavenly Father wants to nurture us.

We can be encouraged by the fact that what has seemed to be impossible is no longer so. Pilgrims on the love journey, who have tragic stories concerning unsatisfactory parenting, have learned to give God love and receive love in return. In many instances they are receiving love by faith for the first time. Actually, no matter how loved we have been by our earthly fathers, our sin nature still contains fear regarding God. God must reparent each one of us, no matter what our emotional experience with our earthly father has been. Of course, that reparenting process is less difficult in many ways if our fathers have been emotionally present to us. However, it needs to be emphasized that it is not impossible to learn to receive God's love by faith if the father has been absent.

Jerry was a young man whose father was a businessman, a workaholic, in a small town in the South. The business demanded tremendous care, involving Jerry's father many hours a day. During childhood Jerry felt his dad ignored him, for he'd been emotionally vacant. Yet one day in a counseling session Jerry said, "I am seeing that my dad was there for our family by providing financially. He showed his love for us in that respect. Sunday dinner and the hour that folowed were his time with us. He was shy about physically showing his love, but he did the best he could. A common reassurance was, 'I don't want you to fret and worry or be insecure about my inability to provide for you, for I always will. You can relax and feel secure in that. Enjoy being young.'"

Jerry continued, "As I look back, I believe his provision and his moral business practices were the ways he showed love to all of us. We were secure in knowing we would be taken care of each day."

One of the great joys of the Love Exchange is that God begins to reveal the frequency with which our earthly father did indeed love us as children. Obviously we were not always cognizant of that love at the time. His way of expressing love may have been non-articulate or non-physical as Zephaniah 3:17 says, "He will be quiet in his love." Our earthly fathers may have given love with financial security, by being loyal to the family or by practicing upstanding business procedures. However, as a child this was too abstract to be assimilated. Now the Holy Spirit must translate those experiences for us.

Our Course of Action

What course of action do we take if indeed we have wrong impressions of God because our fathers were not the role models they should have been?

1. Instead of speaking the lie that God does not love you, affirm many times a day the truth that he does love you. God loves me! Such an affirmation must come from the will as our emotions are void of such love.

Several years ago my husband began repeating the truth, "God loves me," over and over as he walked to and from work. This continual declaration of the truth began to break in on him. Then his loving heavenly Father reassured my husband that he indeed loved him. The message came in a unique way that could be received by him and was an expression of love in itself.

2. Each day in your quiet time with God, have some exchange of love (as outlined in Chapter 2). Though it may seem unsatisfactory to do so without emotion, take at least two minutes to express aloud your love for God. Also allow a couple of minutes to express aloud some great verse that proclaims his love for you. To continue this pattern by faith three or four minutes a

day is not impossible. Keeping it short and persistent, affirm aloud that God does indeed love you.

3. Find someone with whom you can talk freely and regularly. The intimacy of spiritual direction or counseling will aid you in giving and receiving love. Talking with someone else is a part of God's love and grace in reparenting us.

My mother has been my spiritual guide for years. Out of the development of this relationship of a loving exchange has come a deep desire in me to pass on the principles in Titus 2:3-8 which speaks of the older women guiding and loving the younger women. This is a desperately needed ministry today which should include men as well. Along with my parents many others listened to me and counseled me, all of which enriched my faith. It is also another link in a long generational chain of faith whereby I receive faith from the elders and pass it along to the young (2 Timothy 1:5).

One of my greatest joys is to give spiritual direction. This type of relationship often enriches my own life as well as the one seeking direction. In this relationship I am able to listen with love and prayer, to aid in the interpretation of God's message for direction, to give counsel as needed, to guide in the application of biblical principles, to extend comfort and care. These ministries help to reparent others.

My prayer is that in our church today older men and women will allow God to fill their time with this ministry of spiritual direction and counseling. How healing it is to be a "safe place" for struggling young Christians.

4. Give God permission to reparent you. Meditate on Luke 3:38 and come to know that your lineage goes back to God the Father himself.

5. Immerse yourself in the Gospels. They tell us about God's love through Jesus' life, death and resurrection.

6. Write out eight or ten passages of the love Scriptures where God expresses his love for us (as found in Chapter 2) and memorize these passages. Repeat them often aloud during the Love Exchange and during the day as circumstances will allow. May they become so much a part of you that they become as your own expressions of love. Some of my richest and most renewing Love Exchange experiences have been in common places such as the car, our kitchen or the grocery, because I had these verses impregnated in my heart. Whether they be audible or not is incidental.

7. Give thanks to God daily in the Love Exchange, that you are accepted in the beloved as Ephesians 1:5-6 instructs. I often say, "God loves me and accepts me just as I am. Thank you, thank you Jesus."

8. Write out a short paragraph asserting that you are loved by God and repeat it often. An example of this might be:

"My child, I love you so totally, so completely, so eternally; you are my beloved, my beautiful, wonderful child. There is nothing you can do to cause me to stop loving you. You are precious to me, I love you *insert name.*"

9. Practice these exercises:

a. See yourself as the little child you were around the ages of four to eight. See yourself on Jesus' lap and he is loving that little child. Hold that image for several minutes. Let him speak words of love to you as that little child. Say aloud what you believe Jesus would say to you.

b. See your adult self loving your little child. Use your imagination to envision that you are holding in your adult lap your little child, and you're loving that little child. Make these scenes as clear as possible. Relax in this scene and hold it in your mind and heart as long as you can. Speak words of love aloud to your little child.

c. Let conversation of love acceptance flow from the adult to the child, also from Jesus to the child. Receive God's love into your real self, that part of you that is made like him, the you that is radiant and beautiful in Jesus.

Many writers stress letting God love the rejected parts of ourselves, our dark side, our broken, wounded selves. In the Love Exchange we allow, by faith, his love to flow into all parts of us.

A great truth of spiritual growth is that it is possible to obtain spiritual nourishment without being consciously aware of it. In other words, by faith with no emphasis on feeling our emotions, we are nourished and matured. It is God's responsibility to penetrate his love to the various layers of our consciousness.

Wrong Concept of God

A second barrier, which also cripples and hinders any reception of God's love, is the wrong concept of God as being hateful and vengeful. Such an understanding has God always ready to "get" us, to punish us or to do us in. An emotionally deprived childhood spawns such conceptions. It also leaves us with the fear that God is waiting "to hit us with a big stick" if we do not measure up to his standards. Revenge is the name of his game, and he is impossible to please.

Perceptions such as these limit our ability even to sit down in his presence alone, much less go through any ritual of love. Fear of God establishes a powerful barrier to the reception of his love. Frankly, we do not love him at all.

Where our concept of God has been distorted due to extensive abuse from our earthly father, it is difficult to receive divine love. How can we love our heavenly Father when we consider the way our earthly father has acted toward us? Such fear can only be corrected with extensive counseling and spiritual nurturing. This combination allows for the healing of those wounds inflicted on us in the past, while at the same time it allows our relationship with our heavenly Father to be reestablished.

However, if there has not been *extensive abuse* (either sexual or physical) or *excessive emotional privation (for which you will need serious counseling) the following course of action will help you to see your heavenly Father as the loving father he is*.

Our course of action:

1. Start right where you are with your real feelings toward God. Be your real self to get in touch with your feelings. The Love Exchange must come out of deep honesty. Frequently before the exchange with God can take place, you must "Pour our your heart [your emotions] before him" (Psalm 62:8). You may be unable to begin giving or receiving love at the outset. Are you overcome with hurtful and angry feelngs? They must be poured out to God. Such a catharsis is vital to the spiritual journey. Such purging should be a daily undertaking during the beginning of this journey. Many of the great saints of the past have advocated at least a weekly confessional to empty ourselves of sin. It is this *kenosis* or emptying of ourselves that allows us to receive God. With the stress and strain of today's world, a daily time of cleansing is advisable to precede the Love Exchange.

I have many experiences of "pouring out my soul unto the Lord," as Psalm 62:8 suggests. One of the most powerful occurred during an extended period of intense pressure. My schedule included being a full-time student working on my master's degree in marital and family counseling and being a full-time professor at Asbury College. At the same time I was maintaining my prayer life, speaking extensively, teaching a weekly Sunday school class of 130-140 people, keeping our marriage strong and taking care of our home.

The Lord asked me if, by his grace, I could make it through several years of this, being called to bear whatever was necessary for his larger purpose. My reply was yes, and so at the age of 51 I started into a regular schedule of schooling and teaching. I was often pouring out my heart to God in those days, but one episode remains vividly impressed on my mind.

The morning was bright and clear in early spring, and I was scheduled to go to a church in a community near Lexington and lead a prayer seminar lasting the better part of the day.

Awakening early that morning I was exceptionally tired. I did not want to get up to pray, because I knew from past experience that when I was this tired I could not pray. I knew that God understood. I was also angry about leading the day of prayer, because I faced two papers due the next week and important reports the following week. Everything seemed to be coming due at the same time.

The commitment for the day of prayer had been made some time ago, and in no way could I change that, but this did not lessen the burden or make me feel any better.

I found myself praying, "Lord, you have got to help me today or I cannot make it."

As I drove to church I felt totally overwhelmed. My anger level escalated with every mile the more I thought about all I had to do. I surely was not fit to talk about prayer when I did not even want to pray. I was sick and tired of the rat race; it was all too much.

The Lord broke in on my thoughts and said, "See that side road coming up on the right, turn onto it. You have plenty of time to get to the church. You need to tell me all about it out loud. I can take it. I am hurting with you. Just be yourself."

Pulling onto that lovely little country road, I obeyed the Lord absolutely and totally on the spot. I began to speak out loud exactly what I was feeling. I was crying and pounding the steering wheel from time to time, telling it as it was. Sweet relief engulfed me as I took time to pour out my heart to God.

"Lord, I cannot stand this another minute. Your way is too hard. It is killing me, I cannot go on any longer. I absolutely need a break. I am sick of everything I am doing. I am suffocating. I don't even want to pray and that makes me feel awful. I am furious with you and I quit. I cannot go on like this."

Tears were pouring down my face as I got it out of my system. As I came to the end of that tirade, a deep love welled up in my heart for God. I still loved him in the midst of all this.

"Lord, I don't mean all of that, but I am wiped out. I do love you, so much so that I am doing all this crazy stuff for you."

"I know how you feel: I love you and I understand," God responded. "Just relax now. Turn the car around and I am going to pour out my heart of love on you."

As I turned the car around to head back to the main highway, a sense of Jesus became so real I could have reached out and touched him had my spiritual eyes been keener. His love was so present with me. All I felt in those few minutes was a profound overwhelming sense of God loving me. This loving defied articulation and understanding. His love flowed over my heart, mind and soul. My body felt more refreshed than it had in days. Aglow with his love, I pulled back on the main highway a different person. Now I was ready to meet my challenges empowered by the Holy Spirit and enabled by his love. His love always heals our emotional pain, redeems the situation and transforms us.

The impact of this encounter was two-fold. First, perspective was restored to all I had to accomplish in the next weeks and months. The papers, reports, assignments, student recitals, meetings, retreat engagements and all else once again were in the realm of possibility because of God's love for me. I had taken it out of his hands and was attempting to do it all in my own strength. He reminded me that if I persisted in the Love Exchange doing my part, he would fulfill his obligation.

Second, this time of confessional prepared the way for me to become the vessel God needed at the meeting to which I was headed. I was reminded of 2 Corinthians 2:14. "But thanks be to God, who always leads us in His triumph in Christ, and manifests through us the sweet aroma of the knowledge of Him in every place."

God led me to tell those people my experience that occurred on the way to their church that morning. I confessed the whole experience and how gloriously God responded to my honesty. The result of that confessional was the manifesting of Jesus in an unusual way in that meeting that Saturday morning. In other words, "the sweet aroma of the knowledge of Him" was released in that place.

As those dear people listened, they sensed his presence of love. The response was overwhelming with

96

many weeping and acknowledging they needed him to renew them too. The power of our honest pouring out to God was actualized in all of us. We need the cleansing that comes when we tell it like it is!

2. Is there pain and stress in your life, compounded by years of denying your feelings? Do you feel there is no relief or that God cannot get to you? If so, find someone with whom you can talk out those deepest feelings. Often a Christian counselor or therapist is necessary as it will take time even to get in touch with your feelings. Sometimes a spiritual director or a consecrated friend can be a clear channel. "Therefore, confess your sins to one another, and pray for one another, so that you may be healed. The effective prayer of a righteous man can accomplish much" (James 5:16). This imperative is basic to clearing our hearts so Jesus may enter.

3. If you are not on a real spiritual journey, begin at once. Invite God to reveal himself to you and begin seeking divine love. Ask Jesus to come to you. "You will seek Me and find Me, when you search for Me with all your heart" (Jeremiah 29:13).

We can be so non-nurtured by our earthly fathers that we project on God the same non-nurturing qualities. If our earthly fathers have been emotionally or physically abusive, we probably feel real fear about coming to God. We are afraid that he might "strike" us, or ignore us.

Paul says in Hebrews 10:31, "It is a terrifying thing to fall into the hands of the living God." Even if our upbringing has presented God as love through our earthly father, there is natural fear about coming to God. We feel uncertain about what he might do.

If you cannot enthusiastically love God, at least give him two minutes to express to him the appreciation that you are alive and that he is helping you seek him all you can at this time. Thank him for the blessings you have received and allow him time to show you what he is truly like. Read one of the love verses and listen as he speaks to you. Do not let yourself be discouraged or impatient. As you think on the truth of God's love for you, you will be helped enormously and he will gradually and imperceptively alter your inner reality about him. *Do not give up!*

Our Lifestyle

Lifestyle itself can be a barrier. Our lives are frantic, so overextended that we are busy beyond expression. We are too anxious and too nervous to stop and learn to confront God. We are literally too exhausted to add another duty to our schedule. To stop, relax and offer expressions of love to God will take intense effort on our part as we begin. To spend time with God will always require concentrated effort because of our overloaded schedules.

Our Course of Action:

1. No matter how brief the Love Exchange might be, this is still a transforming act when done daily in a quiet time and in our hearts, silently, as we go through the day. This allows God permission to begin to restore us in him.

2. Paul said he had necessities, things he must do. We are not unlike him in our world today. What we call necessities unfortunately spill over into what Chapter 4 of Mark calls the cares of this world. Such twentieth-

century pressures produce the exhausted society of which we are a part—the society too tired to pray. Ask God to show you how to simplify your life all you can by setting your priorities and putting him first. If you cannot spare 15 to 20 minutes a day for a devotional time, you are probably intentionally keeping busy for a purpose. This is to avoid facing yourself and God.

3. As we continue in the Love Exchange (as outlined in Chapter 2), we allow God to get at our deepest need. Running within a frenzied schedule or seeking to get our needs met in other ways begins to wane because *God is meeting our needs*. Knowing we are accepted by God, we find our real worth in him. We do not need to cram our lives so full of activity. We can relax, be still and hear him guide us more in what is best for us to do. We allow God to protect us emotionally and physically.

Lack of Discipline in the Holy Habits

Another barrier is the lack of training from childhood about the necessity for daily discipline in the holy habits. Perhaps we have stressed the big experiences such as rebirth, our initial Love Exchange, to the exclusion of daily partaking of his divine nature. In rebirth we cry out, confessing our sins, and God pours out his loving forgiveness. In the total consecration of our lives, what some call the infilling of his Spirit, God pours out his Spirit in a baptism of love for our cleansing and power.

In its teachings today, the church is stressing not only these major experiences but also the need for daily interaction with God. The daily practice of meeting him in the discipline of prayer and Bible reading is our means of growth. Why? Because we learn to interact with him in love in the daily Love Exchange. Here is where the transformation of our inner needs is brought about. Here we learn to allow him the freedom to work in us.

In response to our willingness to receive his love, God is able to express his love in even deeper ways. The receiving of his love enables us then to walk in his Spirit of love and not in our own strength. Our capacity to receive his love deepens as we continually pour our love on him. Experiencing this infilling of God's love and our loving him in return, the Love Exchange, we are then encouraged to continue our daily walk with him and to reach out to others in love.

Our Course of Action:

1. Begin expressing to God your love for him all through the day. Write out one of the love verses so that you can refer to it during the day.

2. Look over your schedule and find at least ten minutes for a quiet time to experience the Love Exchange daily. Be as regular as you can.

3. Discuss the busyness of your schedule with someone and discover why you are so overextended. Be accountable to that person for your quiet time.

Living Out of the False Self

Living out of the false self and not knowing who I really am in God, is the result of poor self-esteem. This is a serious barrier, but I am seeing people grow in loving themselves as they begin to find out God loves them.

Psalm 4:4 says, ". . . commune with your own heart upon your bed, and be still." In other words, there is an act of getting in touch with myself, a process where I grow in self-knowledge about who I am.

We take to our false selves because we do not like who we really are. The Love Exchange brings God's love to us so we can deal with ourselves. The pain of our sinfulness, our fears of losing control, our dark sides are all dealt with to the degree we allow God to heal them. The Love Exchange helps the individual face the defense mechanisms employed to evade the truth about himself as he daily receives God's love. By his Spirit he empowers us to face the truth about ourselves as Psalm 51:6 and 17 says. Self-acceptance begins to take over self-hate as we accept our emptiness before God and see how he loves us in spite of our pride, vanity and pettiness. His love does not let us be overwhelmed, but rather we begin to know we are truly accepted in him.

The giving out of love to God and receiving his love in return is the most needed and most healing experience we can have.

Our Course of Action:

1. Barriers in our psychological makeup can be acute. With a qualified Christian therapist, a network system of support, a daily time with God that stretches us into an ever deepening Love Exchange, miracles can and do happen. Where there is neurosis or mental illness there must be qualified professional help.

2. Continue on the Love Exchange journey as prescribed in Chapter 2.

3. Refuse to allow yourself discouragement or impatience.

4. Write a paragraph of "God Talk" and use it during the day. Examples might include: "You are so precious to me," and "I love you with an everlasting love."

5. Bathe daily in all of the love verses, say them aloud, and seek to accept their message by faith.

Self-Hate

If during childhood an individual has not been nurtured by the parents and other family members, the child feels worthless and has no sense of value as a person. He comes to hate himself. The message has not been received that it is normal to like ourselves. The fact that there is no acceptance of self is reflected in turn in negative self-talk. Not being able to like ones-self certainly prohibits any belief that our heavenly Father could love us.

Shelia was brought up in a family that was so tense no one could relax emotionally. Both parents worked and would dash home in the evenings to throw a meal on the table, cram clothes in the washer and dryer, take care of the three youngest children and totally ignore and neglect Shelia. She began to feel something was wrong with her. She deduced that she must not be a worthy person because her parents only gave attention to the other three children. She fended for herself and rarely had interaction with either parent. Her evaluation of her situation was that since they did not seem to find her lovable enough to show her love she evidently was not lovable.

This carried over into her adult life and she felt a deep dislike for herself. Her parents relayed a false truth that she was not worthy of being noticed. She had difficulty believing God could notice her if her parents failed to do so.

Sheila started the Love Exchange cautiously, but willing to give it a chance. With therapy and a devotional life in motion, she moved into a journey of discovering God had a message for her, a message very different from her parents' message—of being constantly overlooked to one where she was noticed and appreciated.

Our Course of Action:

1. Possible therapy with a qualified therapist.

2. Institute the Love Exchange as a part of your devotional time.

3. Write out three or four scripture verses which speak to you of God's love for you, using them as a point of meditation. Say them aloud many times during the day. As you breath, begin to realize that you are breathing in God's love for you.

4. Accept your past and begin to take it to the cross—piece by piece. Forgiveness is a process. Under the guidance of a Christan counselor move from one instance of hurt to another, always claiming the forgiveness of God by faith.

5. Self-hate produces rebellion toward the ones who have hurt us and toward God. Know that the Talionic Impulse (I will do to others what they have done to me) must be laid down. "You have heard that it was said, 'An eye for an eye, and a tooth for a tooth.' You have heard that it was said, "You shall love your neighbor, and hate your enemy." But I say to you, love your enemies, and pray for those who persecute you'" (Matthew 5:38-48).

Conclusion

Our ability through meditation on God's word and our faith to be able to receive or respond to God's love is definitely part of our emotional condition. We all have emotional hangups from childhood that prevent us from perceiving God as love. Our earthly father may have exhibited cruelty and totally nonrelational behavior toward us as children. We, in turn, project on God these misconceptions learned at an early age from a parent who did not function properly. A person of this persuasion will have a long journey, but the Love Exchange will be worth the trip. To learn the truth about God—that he truly loves us and we can live out of that truth—is what heals us and corrects the past misconceptions of God.

To activate one's faith by truly "hearing" the truth of God's love for us is part and parcel of the Love Exchange. That ceremony of giving the love we have, no more and no less, is allowing the Holy Spirit to begin the healing process within us. We learn to dwell in the truth of John 3:16. As we concentrate our energies on the eternal truth of God's love, his love will begin its healing process.

I realize some people are so damaged they can barely sit in God's presence. But if they are willing to go with Jesus on this journey, there can be help for them. At some point reinforcement is needed to complete the help given by their counselor or therapist—a short time, maybe six or seven minutes a day of meditation on God's word. The love passages will shed new light on God's heart, plus revealing the tragic consequences of sin. We will begin to see that our sinful and fallen world is a place where we are sinned against and we, in turn, operate under the impulse to get even. We retaliate and sin against those who have hurt us. The whole world lies in the power of the evil one (1 John 5:19).

The Love Exchange provides a way to "overcome evil with good" as Paul says, "Do not be overcome by evil, but overcome evil with good" (Romans 12:21).

Receiving by faith God's love is the only way for God's grace to heal. In the Love Exchange that healing is facilitated by daily affirmation of the truth of all truths—*God loves me!* Our earthly parents may not have loved us, but the truth is God does and always will love us. This is the foundation for all healing.

એ•ભ

The amazing fruits
of abiding in obedience
to the love commandments
are answers to prayer
that will literally drop off
the trees of intercession.

એ•ભ

Chapter 6

How the Love Exchange Affects Others

But we all, with unveiled face beholding as in a mirror the glory of the Lord, are being transformed into the same image from glory to glory, just as from the Lord, the Spirit.

2 Corinthians 3:18

The church soloist at my father's church sang with great zeal, "Thou shalt love the Lord thy God, love him with all thy heart, all thy soul, and all thy strength." I was just a little tyke at the time, but I remember that as the words seemed to soar to the rafters so did my heart. *How wonderful it would be to love God that way. My parents had taught me to love God, and now this beautiful song was encouraging me to do the same. Someday, I shall love him that way, I would dream. Someday I'm going to love him exactly like the words say.* From those early words of encouragement, my lifetime aspiration has become to love God in such an unreserved way.

Years later as I reflect on the journey in which Jesus has led me, I know many miles still remain, but oh the fulfilling peace of the love journey. Today I love him as never before, and as I continue to love him, he increases my love for him and others.

Out of my own experience I have come to believe that the requirement of Matthew 22:34-40 is possible for us all. "But when the Pharisees heard that He had put the Sadducees to silence, they gathered themselves together. And one of them, a lawyer, asked Him a question, testing Him, 'Teacher, which is the great commandment in the Law?' And He said to him, 'You shall love the Lord your God with all your heart, and with all your soul, and with all your mind.' This is the great and foremost commandment. The second is like it, 'You shall love your neighbor as yourself.' On these two commandments depend the whole Law and the Prophets.'" Very little has been taught concerning obedience to the love commandments. The result then is that today many Christians do not believe biblical love, divine love, is even possible in their lives. And if it *is* possible, how can it be actualized in their lives?

The annals of church history are full of people who have dared to love God with a totality which has made a lasting contribution to the Christian experience. Our tendency, however, is to think only special or great Christians can ever fulfill this requirement. This is not so. These great souls were people like you and me at the outset of their walk. They caught a vision of what they could become with the love of God in their hearts, and then they set out to make that vision a reality.

One of the principal lessons we learn in the Love Exchange is that we cannot love God as we should in our human love. It is God's love, the love shed abroad in us by the Holy Spirit, that is the love we offer up to him.

The first chapters of this book are aids in teaching us how to love God with all our heart, soul and mind. Also included in these chapters is how we allow him to love us. Quickly the discovery is made in the Love Exchange that our unloving attitudes toward others hinder the flow of God's love in us. With an unfolding awareness of how real his love is for us, we discover new attitudes emerging towards those who for us have been so unlovable. The dawning reality is that we can no longer harbor unforgiving thoughts toward others and expect any reality or honesty in the Love Exchange.

The First Epistle of John is quite explicit about this love relationship with God and others. Look at four of these verses: "Beloved, if God so loved us, we also ought to love one another . . . . We love, because he first loved us. If someone says, 'I love God,' and hates his brother, he is a liar; for the one who does not love his brother whom he has seen, cannot love God whom he has not seen. And this commandment we have from Him, that the one who loves God should love his brother also" (1 John 4:11, 19-21).

To illustrate these truths I relate a personal experience of how the transforming power of the Love Exchange worked on my attitude toward others. Several years ago, while deeply involved in the Love Exchange, my love for God and his love for me was so vital and comforting. But along side this encounter I was sensing my attitudes of anger, jealousy and envy toward three women acquaintances. Such attitudes restrained me from letting his love flow out of me to others in prayer, and they hindered the flow of my love to him. He could not allow me to keep loving him while continuing in such judgmental attitudes toward these three women.

In my prayers for them, which were shallow and infrequent, I imposed demands on God to change *them*. My mother calls this "being on God's Advisory Board or acting as general manager of the universe," telling God what to do and when to do it. But God made it clear that I did not even have good will toward them, much less love. As a part of that revelation he showed me that divine love at its lowest level is good will toward everyone. There cannot be one person toward whom I am permitted to exhibit ill will. I must want only what is good for them and wish them no ill at all.

God disclosed to me that his love flowing through me in prayer and any right attitudes of love were blocked by a log jam of harmful attitudes. I was being highly selective in my love of others. Inside my love would shut down, but on the outside I acted nice to those I did not like. As God loved me that day he asked if I were willing to allow his divine love to begin working in those negative qualities of criticism, judgment and complaining. Then and only then could his love flow out of me to others.

Great remorse swept over me at the discovery of my harsh and critical temperament. When I cried out, "God, do whatever you need to do to cleanse me and let your love flow," he drew me to Matthew 5:43-48. 'You have heard that it was said, 'You shall love your neighbor, and hate your enemy.' But I say to you, love your enemies, and pray for those who persecute you in order that you may be sons of your Father who is in heaven; for He causes His sun to rise on the evil and the good, and sends rain on the righteous and the unrighteous. For if you love those who love you, what reward have you? Do not even the tax-gatherers do the same? And if you greet your brothers only, what do you do more than others? Do not even the Gentiles do the same? Therefore you are to be perfect, as your heavenly Father is perfect." Here I saw how to love those that are hard to love, my enemies, those who bother me or persecute me. The divine formula was right there—so simple, so powerful. What is a formula but a prescription or recipe which followed will produce certain guaranteed results? Conditions are to be met, with inevitable consequences, but we must go to our guide book, the Bible, which gives the directions. The divine formula as stated above begins with honest prayer for those we find hard to love. As we pray for the unlovable then we begin to receive God's divine love for others.

My meditation on these verses was not over yet, when I heard God say, "I want you to start praying for these women, with good will for them. As you pray for them more than yourself, I will begin to give you my divine love for them. As you begin to love them, your prayers for them will come from the heart."

I answered honestly, "I cannot obey this right now. Maybe next year I will be more mature in God's love and can love them then. I need to 'work my way up' to Matthew 5:44."

"No, you do not work your way up to loving as you should. While you obey and begin to pray I will give you my love for these women now," came his words of encouragement.

"Alright, I'll try. Lord, bless them," I prayed. Silence from me and from heaven followed.

"Is that all you are going to say?" came the reply.

"Well, bless them a lot," was my matter of fact answer.

"Yes, go on. Can you pray that with more feeling?"

"Well, bless their children," I continued.

"Isn't that rather general?"

"Well, bless them in unusual ways."

"That is a little better, keep going."

"Lord, I pray you will give every good and perfect gift to these three women."

There was a little more feeling, but I was ashamed of how loveless I was in my praying for them. I was beginning to see that prayer "shows up" how we really feel toward others and that we fail to pray for those we find difficult to love. We simply shut them out.

Finally, out of my heart and my will,I felt a yearning over them and said, "Oh Lord, manifest your presence in their lives, reveal yourself to them more than to me." The words seemed to tremble in the air and my emotions were unsettled, but my will felt at peace.

"That's more like it, you're on the right track. You'll receive more and more of my love as you continue to confront your real feelings and be more specific in prayer for these three children of mine."

"Lord, it's hard to pray where it's hard to love. It's difficult to pray even with good will when you don't care. After all, these women have hurt me, they haven't been nice."

Then the Lord helped me to remember the time when I had not been nice to them and others.

"Oh, Lord, I do want to do this, to please you. I know you! Let's go at it again tomorrow. I love you."

What an adventure that was—to seek to pray for these women. As the days and weeks went by, I felt an increase in my caring mingled somehow with God's caring. I began to see them more as he saw them and to feel his compassion stirring in me.

Three or four weeks later as I was lifting them in prayer one morning, a tremendous surge of compassion, identification and real honest-to-God caring for this trio engulfed me. The prayer that sprang up from my heart was a prayer of his love expressing real care for them and their families. Caught up in the thrill and amazement of it all I heard myself exclaim, "Lord, you are so good, you are so precious, you are wonderful." Matthew 5:44 really works just as you said. As I've prayed daily for them, you have given me your love so that I now truly care. Your love is amazing! Prayer is an open door into your heart of love."

As we pray for those hard to love prayer opens the door for God's love to be realized in our hearts. With no prayer there is no realizing of divine love. Prayer opens the door to Jesus, who is love (Revelation 3:20,21).

God's response to my insight came: "I will pour out my love because you've actually been praying more for them than yourself. I always answer prayer like that. You're beginning to care with my caring and forgetting about yourself a little."

"Why Lord, I now find it easy to pray for them. It's a pleasure. I really care. I feel your love and my love all mixed together."

"Yes, I love that," God answered, "You've prayed yourself into my love for them which causes you to love them too."

The amazing thing was that his love for me was never sweeter or more real than during that prayer experiment. Nothing seems to please God more than when we take his commandments to love seriously.

As the days and weeks rolled by, God opened up natural, easy communication with each of these three women, and I began to enjoy seeing them and talking with them. They were really quite wonderful women.

At the beginning, I was praying for God to change *them*. Naturally, I had assumed they were the ones who needed to be changed and not me. But to my amazement, I could see and feel an unbelievable change in me. A super-critical spirit had pervaded my response to them in the past, but now as I became better acquainted with them my judgment and criticism waned. I could no longer judge them for I was investing too much in praying and loving them. Criticism had been checked in my spirit. No longer could I look with a critical eye at these newly-found friends. Criticism had become so repugnant that even to hear others criticize them was distressing to me.

What rare changes prayer can make. Learning to love with his love as I prayed caused a glorious thing to take place—as I prayed, I also loved. Evidence shows that you cannot love someone and not pray for him or her. The reverse is also true in that you cannot pray for someone and not love him or her. The loving is the praying and the praying the love. When God is convinced of our intentions to pray for those whom we find difficult to love, he will impart to us his love for them.

Jesus' word to us as found in Matthew 5:44, "love your enemies, and pray for those who persecute you," is more powerful than we realize. Here is established the formula to love and pray, and pray and love. He gives us this admonition so that we can exercise family spiritual traits and resemble our Father's impartial loving. Our brothers and sisters, who make up the potential family of God, may make our lives difficult, but it is imperative that we remember them as brothers and sisters and let nothing stop the flow of love and prayer. The trait of impartial love which belongs to our Father must be ours as we love those we find difficult to love and those we find easy to love.

When we are walking in obedience to this prayer-love formula, our actions become more closely related to the impartiality of God's love. We become sons or daughters of the most high God as we take this formula and incorporate it into our living. To begin, we pray for his love for them to be manifested in us. Simultaneously we move from a feeling of good will into dimensions of real caring for the unlovable. As we learn to love with his kind of love we begin to experience a maturing, multi-dimensional divine love for others. We do not suddenly burst in on this mature kind of loving. Such mature love is the distinct result of praying for those difficult to love and those who make things difficult for us. Here our family characteristics are vividly demonstrated.

This maturing process allows God access into our lovelessness towards him and others. I firmly believe that what initiates the maturing or perfecting love process is loving those hard to love. We want to love only "our kind" of people. But God says you cannot grow or mature in love until you begin praying to love the hard to love. Probably our most needed prayer list is the list of those we find difficult to love and who make life difficult for us.

I believe it is only in this kind of prayer that we begin to experience divine love in new dimensions. The human tendency is to *talk* about those who are hard to love and then we most often *pray* very little. When others are hard to love, we shut down, get fed up and say, "We're through."

But Matthew 5:44—"I [Jesus] say to you, love your enemies, and pray for those who persecute you"— declares we are not showing our family trait of love or evidencing a growth in God's love unless we continue to pray for the unlovable and those who make life difficult for us.

Sometimes we give up too soon on those hard to love; sometimes we never even begin. We must ask ourselves,

"Is there someone in my life to whom I've stopped giving love? Is there someone from whom I have withdrawn my love?" Thank God, Jesus doesn't give up on loving us!

To return to my experience, the miracle continued to unfold, for over a period of time two of these three women are now among my closest friends. The third relationship has never been allowed to grow as she has since moved out of town. I still pray for her and feel the time will come for our friendship to be renewed. However, I love her with God's love and will always love her.

As this tremendous experiment of the divine formula (Matthew 5:43-48) was going on over a period of months, God cultivated a passion to keep the flow of his love activated in me. I began to see that staying in God's love, not only in times of prayer but all through the day, is the very essence of the gospel. Did not Jesus say "Just as the Father has loved Me, I have also loved you; abide in my love" (John 15:9). Live in his love regardless of the cost. Allow nothing to lure us away from that love. Paul reiterates this in his glorious words from Romans 8:37-39, telling us not to allow anything or anybody to separate us from his love for us."

I became aware of the fact that all daily interactions are opportunities to stay in his love. To say yes to the love commandment of abiding, living in that love, means to remain in the Love Exchange constantly, all through the day.

I experienced the dawning reality that "because the love of God has been poured out within our hearts through the Holy Spirit who was given to us" (Romans 5:5), by his power we can stay in divine love. This is our privilege—to abide in his glorious love with which he endues us in the Love Exchange, not only in those minutes of our quiet time but all through the day.

We are enabled to stay in that divine love by obeying the love commandments, as found throughout Chapters 13-17 of the gospel of John. When our response of love is obedience to these all important love commandments we begin to grow and mature in God's love. We find no contentment in merely existing in the understanding of divine love that we experienced when we were born again or even filled with his Spirit, much less our understanding of years ago. The real joy now is in an ever-growing reality of his love nature. The necessity of saying yes to all his lessons in divine love is a given. If we are to learn to abide in that divine love, we must take the lessons as they come.

We will find ourselves saying, "Thank you, God, for sending me Jane Q. She is so obnoxious and very difficult to love, but I realize now that you knew I needed her. I need her as another lesson in loving the unlovable. You want to work in me and in her at the same time."

I began studying the word for the divine formulas which could enable me to remain in God's love according to John 15:7, "If you abide in Me, and My words abide in you, ask whatever you wish, and it shall be done for you." The implication is that prayers are answered as I obey his love commandments. What are these love commandments? Where are they in the Word of God and what do they mean? How important are they, and how can I get my life in alignment with them?

Often shortly before a man dies he will speak the most important words of his life. The Gospel of John records the last words of Jesus as he faced the cross. Following the washing of the disciples' feet and Judas leaving the Upper Room, Jesus gives one of his most profound directives: "A new commandment I give to you, that you love one another, even as I have loved you, that you also love one another. By this all men will know that you are My disciples, if you have love for one another" (John 13:34-35). Here we have a commandment from Jesus. If a commandment is an order with no option, do we then have a choice in abiding by it? We may say that it sounds too demanding, but would Jesus have given us an order that is beyond our capabilities? I think not. Jesus knows us better than we ourselves and therefore would not require something unreasonable of us. Remember, he loves us. Would someone who loves us ask of us the impossible?

Profound changes are possible when we move out in love as this commandment of Jesus reads. The reverse is also true—that our lives can't see the power of God's love if we say no to the love commandments.

A young college student had just heard my message on loving others and asked, "Mrs. Therkelsen, what if I don't want to obey the love commandments?"

My answer was simply, "You are not moving in obedience and therefore not walking with Jesus" (1 John 1:3-7).

The response of this student is typical of much of our world today when it comes to loving those we find so difficult to love. While she was speaking out of her youthful immaturity, this student's response is typical of most failures. As she matures she may see that she must learn to love as Jesus has commanded or she will be destroyed. Her life will be full of people difficult to love, and she will be a difficult person to love also.

Actually, to go the "love way" is the easy way to live, even as 1 John 5:3 says. His commandments of love are not burdensome; they are a way of victory. I have found that when I refuse to love the path is harder than when I chose to love with his love, which restrains my selfishness. With his love we move into life rather than death (1 John 3:14).

This whole formula breaks down when we refuse to take the first step and say yes to what God has asked us to do. The loving response will not come of its own accord. If we refuse to avail ourselves of the empowerment of prayer our attitudes cannot be changed. The most serious laws of the land are these love commandments, and we probably sin against the love commandments more than any other of God's laws. The main issue for us is whether or not we will be obedient and take seriously his words concerning love.

Jesus is saying in John 13:34 that we are to love even as he loves us which is the indication that we belong to him. His divine love flowing through this people is the witness to the world that we are his people. In other words, the criterion is not baptism, tongues, church membership, or anything else, only the divine love of Jesus flowing among his children. "Oh, how they love one another," was the comment made of the early church. What a tragedy that our distinguishing mark today is not the "even as" love, because we fail to love "even as" he has loved us. The negligence on our part to enter into this godly way of loving results in the world's inability to know we belong to Jesus.

We spend thousands of dollars on improving our witness skills with few results to show for the time and money expended. Even with all of this we have failed to hear what Jesus says about the inevitable result of learning to love with "even as" love or God's love flowing through us. We fall into judgment and criticism, rather than obeying the divine formula of Matthew 5:43-48 of praying and loving with his love. "Even as" love is releasing his mighty Calvary love with all it's healing properties, the world can say nothing in return. It is his love in us that convinces them Jesus is the Son, and we are truly his disciples.

Go on to Chapter 14 of the Gospel of John and see the love commandments there. "If you love me you will keep my commandments" (v.15). Jesus is again reinforcing our deep need for obedience. Obedience then becomes the love, and how much we love him is revealed in how obedient we are to him. It could be summed up by saying that obedience is the spiritual discipline of love. The above verse is saying that love is keeping the commandments to love even as he loved me. It means keeping the love commandments when I do not want to; when it is difficult; when my emotions are raging; when to love as he loves me costs me more than I planned on; when self rises to defend itself and I could care less about loving or I only want my way. These then are some of the times when my *will must make a choice to love with this love in spite of angry emotions* (1 John 3:18).

John continues in Chapter 14 with the amazing promises of God to those who resolve to love as he loves, regardless of the cost to the self-life with all of its justifications. The theme is to die to ourselves so his love can come forth. "If you love Me, you will keep My commandments. "He who has My commandments and keeps them, he it is who loves Me ; and he who loves Me shall be loved by My Father, and I will love him, and will disclose Myself to him . . . . "If anyone loves Me, he will keep My word; and My Father will love him, and We will come to him, and make Our abode with him. He who does not love Me does not keep my words; and the word which you hear is not Mine, but the Father's who sent me . . . . "But that the world may know that I love the Father, and as the Father gave Me commandment, even so I do." (verses 15, 21, 23-24, 31).

What amazing words are found here. These words urge us into an ever deepening obedience to the love commandments so that our relationship of friendship and oneness with the entire Trinity is possible. I truly believe all growth in the Christian life is dependent on our understanding how to grow, how to be increasingly more open and receptive to him. Obedience to the love commandments of Jesus is the "how to" of growth. He is so pleased when we are obedient to the "even as" love because it releases him to come closer and closer to us, so we can be better friends. These priceless words that Jesus spoke facing his arrest and the cross are the "how to" of all Christian growth and experience.

Look at these verses slowly and carefully. Jesus reaffirms that genuine love of him is obedience to what he says about loving others. "If you love Me, you will keep My commandments" (v. 15). Loving Jesus and others is not a series of emotional highs, warm fuzzies, or a surge of emotional love at unexpected times, in the quiet time or even during a church service. These experiences have their place, but the real test of how much we love Jesus is how strongly our will is fixed to obey him. Our selfish human way of loving with all its partiality and selectivity is laid aside. Our will chooses his kind of love that is impartial and non-selective. Our will resolves to love with his love no matter how difficult the situation.

The wonderful thing about God's love is that he will protect me from others and myself. Many people feel God's love means we allow ourselves to be abused by others. But God's love is so creative. He will often say through us as we speak the truth in love (Ephesians 4:15): "I cannot allow you to speak to me or hurt me in this way because I am loved by God." Other times, in physical or sexual abuse, divine love will remove us from those situations. In still other times God will have me say nothing or do nothing. Obedience opens the door for him to speak and do what is best in that particular situation.

In John 14:21 the rewards of this kind of love—obedience or we could say will-obedience (not emotional up and down obedience)—is absolutely beyond our wildest imagination. Jesus himself says that if we will obey his commandments to love with his love, he will come and live with us. Our obedience will release Jesus to be more and more himself with us, revealing his nature, personality and life. The potentiality for a friendship beyond anything we have ever known hinges on my surrender to his laws of love.

Jesus can only reveal himself in a loving environment. As I obey his love commandments he allows me to "see" and "hear" him in amazing ways. If we fail to say yes to loving as he loves, Jesus is not free to show us himself and how he acts. Intimacy is nurtured in disclosure. We prohibit him from being free to "come alive" in us and through us when we say no to the love commandments. When we harbor ill will, unforgiveness and resentments of human love and refuse to pray until his love flows through us to those hard to love, we cannot grow in knowing him. Jesus will become more and more real to us if we say yes to the commandments of love.

But these verses reveal even more of what is possible for the obedient Christian. John 14:23 says, "If anyone loves Me, he will keep My word; and My Father will love him, and we will come to him, and make our abode with him."

Imagine, not only may we have a deepening friendship with Jesus if we are obedient to the love laws, but also a deepening friendship with God our heavenly Daddy. When I need Daddy, he will be living in my spirit "house" and I can run to him. When I need Jesus, my elder brother, my Savior, he is available to me. Can it be true? 1 John 4:12 says no one has seen God at any time, but if we love one another God abides in us and shows himself as we love one another.

In the past several years the renewal movement has needfully and powerfully stressed that the Holy Spirit wants to be in us rather than only with us. "He abides with you, and will be in you" (John 14:17). We had wandered so far from the reality of God's inner presence as our source of empowerment to love that this message has sometimes been viewed as almost an end in itself. Get the Holy Spirit within and that is it. We have it all.

The reality of John 14:21 and 23 is that there is a relationship of intimacy with God and Jesus and the Holy Spirit that has far-reaching potential for fulfillment beyond my wildest dreams. I will begin to realize the roles of each Person of the Trinity in an ever more intimate way if I will move in loving obedience to his love commandment to love others as he has loved me. Incredible! The entire Trinity can be living inside me and available to me if I say yes to loving even as God loves.

The wonder of these verses from John 14 is that God hungers and longs to reveal himself to us, and that disclosure is necessary to grow together in love. For many people Jesus and the Holy Spirit may be real, but God seems too stern and too removed. John 14:23 reaffirms that God the Father wants a warm, loving, caring relationship with us. He longingly waits to show us what a wonderful parent he is. As we move into the love adventure he becomes more lovingly real.

I believe Jesus discloses himself in this love covenant in two ways. First, he wants to uncover his love response in all our personal, one-to-one Love Exchange encounters. The Love Exchange is one way we allow him to bring to light his true loving nature. Second, Jesus wants to make known his love response in all the interactions, conversations and reactions of our daily lives. How this unfolds we will discuss later, but for now know that it is our will that responds to others when we say yes to love. Jesus will reveal to us what words and actions will allow this life-changing love to flow through us. In each time and place he will manifest himself if we allow him.

Paul says it in 2 Corinthians 4:7, "We have this treasure in earthen vessels, that the surpassing greatness of the power may be of God and not from ourselves." This treasure is the Trinity released to love in and through us.

John 14:24 and 31 assures us that Jesus must obey and has obeyed the love commandments of his Father. These commandments come not from Jesus, but it is the Father's plan of reproducing his love nature. There is a line of command: Jesus obeys the Father's command-ments, and we must obey Jesus' commandments. In verse 31 Jesus says, "I love the Father." Jesus' love is also revealed in his obedience as our love level is revealed in our acting out of obedience.

Jesus speaks here of his loving the Father, which I believe is his only time to make this statement. Jesus showed his love of the Father by acting out obedience to the love commandments. Jesus is saying that we must obey the love commandments in our walk as he was obligated to obey them in his walk. As we live a life of obedience it becomes our witness to the world. "The one who says he abides in him ought himself to walk in the same manner as he walked" (1 John 2:6). " A pupil is not above his teacher; but everyone, after he has fully been trained, will be like his teacher" (Luke 6:40). "And why do you call Me, 'Lord, Lord' and do not do what I say?" (Luke 6:46).

Moving on to John 15:9-17 we find the element in the love commandments where Jesus urges us to *live in this divine love of God*. He also shares some of the benefits of this living. "Just as the Father has loved Me, I have also loved you; abide in My love. If you keep My commandments, you will abide in My love; just as I have kept my Father's commandments, and abide in His love. These things I have spoken to you, that My joy may be in you, and that your joy may be full. This is My commandment, that you love one another, just as I have loved you. Greater love has no one that this, that one lay down his life for his friends. You are My friends, if you do what I command you. No longer do I call you slaves, for the slave does not know what his master is doing; but I have called you friends, for all things that I have heard from My Father I have made known to you. You did not choose Me, but I chose you, and appointed you, that you should go and bear fruit, and that your fruit should remain, that whatever you ask of the Father in My name, He may give it to you. This I command you, that you love one another."

From these words of Jesus we begin to see the characteristic of divine love that calls us to lay down our lives, or our way of loving and our way of living. The new life we are now going to be living will be so structured that in every circumstance divine love is released rather than selfish love. In this new life, where our will says yes to his will of love, my obedience to him allows for this change to take place.

A verse by verse examination of this chapter will enable us to see the extent to which our lives will be affected.

Verse 9: As the Father has loved his Son, Jesus, and Jesus has loved us, his brothers and sisters, we are also to live in that flow of divine love back to God and out to others. Paul admonishes the church at Corinth to "pursue love" (1 Corinthians 14:1) or paraphrased, let love be your passion in life. The most urgent call on our Christian walk is remaining in or abiding in the love that Jesus receives from his Father and is passed on to us.

We pour out our best energies in accepting and living what we feel is the good life, not in abiding in the love of God. Our powers are spent and we allow the enemy of our soul to pull us from the abiding place of divine love. This explains so many of our defeats in life. We are living out of his love and living solely in human love, or the flesh.

Paul has determined that nothing is of such consequence as to keep him from God's love. "For I am convinced that neither death, nor life, nor angels, nor principalities, nor things present, nor things to come, nor powers, nor height, nor depth, nor any other created thing, shall be able to separate us from the love of God, which is in Christ Jesus our Lord" (Romans 8:38-39). Nothing, including tragedy and hardship, can get him out of divine love. Oh, could we say this with Paul? Jesus is appealing to us to persist in his love to allow nothing to pull us out of the reality that God loves us and his love is sufficient. What pulls us out of the truth of his love? Is our aim in life the desire to stay in divine love, or rather to pursue prestige, power, security? Our energies have *often* been applied to the wrong journey. I believe Jesus wants our energies to stay in the Love Exchange whether we are in the prayer closet or the market place. Staying in his divine love is seeking his kingdom first, then all other things we need are added.

Verse 10: Jesus obeyed the commandments of God's love as his obedient Son. Should our response to this reflect some preferential treatment? No. You and I must obey as a son or daughter as did God's Son. If we obey his love commandment, we will abide in his love. Obedience to the love commandments is the key, not emotional highs and lows. Is our will fixed on obedience regardless of the circumstances?

Verse 11: Jesus' joy stems from obedience to his Father's love commandments. Our experience of true joy will be the same as Jesus' joy to the degree we are obedient to the love commandments. Joy is the consequence of sharing God's love. That joy is pure and beyond anything the world has to offer! What can compare to the joy of allowing God to flow through us with his holy love?

Verse 12: The fact that the love commandment is restated in this verse and again in verse 17 reinforces the significant nature of its message.

Verse 13: This verse gives us the basic characteristic of divine love. A personal sacrifice of our ways of loving and living must be made in exchange for his ways. This involves a laying down of our understanding and control of our lives, a denial of doing things according to the dictates of human love and understanding.

Verse 14: The focus of the previous verses instructs us as to changes we are to make in our lifestyle. This verse assures us that the result of our obedience will be our growing friendship with God.

Verse 15: Our relationship with God is one of two types. If it is as the slave, the relationship is cold and impersonal. The slave was prohibited from speaking to the master in matters of business or any personal exchange. When such a relationship exists between us and God, there is no intimacy. We're in his vicinity but have no relationship with him.

On the other hand, if we have been obedient to the love commandments, the relationship we have established is that of friends. We share all feelings, concerns, desires. The lines of communication are open as only it can be between friends. Our relationship with God therefore depends on the degree of obedience to the love commandments. Jesus says he will share all things that he has heard from the Father. The type of oneness that is established develops out of a deep personal relationship Jesus wants for each of us.

Jesus reveals more and more of God's plans for bringing about his kingdom of love. Isaiah 45:2,3 says he gives us the treasures of darkness and hidden wealth of secret places. God shares secrets with us as he sees our devotion to his love mature. He sees he can trust us—we are serious about his love nature and we want to be like him.

Verse 16: When obedience to love is our focus, the inevitable result is the miracle of God's love-answers to prayer or fruit that remains. The byproduct of divine love is fruitful prayer. The law of prayer is the law of love. Our focus is to get an answer; God's focus is conforming us to his image by keeping us in his love, then the fruit will fall from the tree of love as a result of obedience to love. We cancel out so much of our praying by failing to obey the love-leadings of the Holy Spirit within us. Our attitudes of resentment, jealousy, anger, unforgiveness cut our prayers short because his love is not there.

The amazing fruits of abiding in obedience to the love commandments are answers to prayer that will literally drop off the trees of intercession—ripe, beautiful answers, his answers to prayers from hearts in harmony with the love commands. "Whatever you ask of the Father in My name, He may give to you" (John 15:16). In other words, answers come easily as a byproduct of our being obedient to his love commandments.

So much of our praying is outside that obedience to love. We are praying amiss. As James 4:3 says, "You ask and do not receive, because you ask with the wrong motives, so that you may spend it on your pleasures." But whatever we ask in his name or nature, whatever we ask dwelling in his love nature he can reward with answers.

The benefits we will enjoy in this love relationship continue in John 16:26-27. "In that day you will ask in My name, and I do not say to you that I will request the Father on your behalf; for the Father himself loves you, because you have loved me, and have believed that I came forth from the Father."

Here we are given the assurance of direct access to God the Father and his love. This assurance reinforces what was stated in John 14:23. "If anyone loves me, he will keep my word; and my Father will love him, and we will come to him, and make our abode with him." God, our Father of love, greets us with open arms during prayer because we honor him by our obedience.

The promise of God's blessings to those who are obedient has roots in the Old Testament. We recall that God's word to his people as highlighted in Deuteronomy chapters 6, 7 and 30 is much the same. "In that I command you today to love the Lord your God, to walk in His ways and to keep His commandments and His statues and His judgments, that you may live and multiply, and that the Lord your God may bless you in the land where you are entering to possess it." Deuteronomy 30:16.

God loves us when we love Jesus. Thus is the theme of the last of the love commandments found in John 17:21-23, 26. "That they may all be one; even as Thou; Father, art in Me, and I in Thee, that they also may be in Us; that the world may believe that thou didst send

Me. And the glory which Thou hast given Me I have given to them; that they may be one, just as We are one; I in them, and Thou in Me, that they may be perfected in unity, that the world may know that thou didst send Me, and didst love them, even as Thou didst love Me. And I have made Thy name known to them, and will make it known; that the love wherewith Thou didst love Me may be in them, and I in them."

What an awesome realization to know that God loves you and me, even as God loves Jesus! The Trinity is inclusive in their divine love as they reach down and include you and me in their love. The very love that they have for one another is to be experienced and shared with us as we are obedient to the love commandment. This very sharing of God's love is what convinces the world Jesus is the Son of God. What amazing love to include you and me in the same love the Trinity has for one another.

Though we are allowed to partake of the love emanating from the Trinity, we are also given the responsibility to carry that love to others in the fulfilling of the love commandments. As contemporary disciples we are obliged to allow Jesus to make known the love nature of our Father through us. He will make it known every time we permit him to manifest himself as we obey the love commandments. "And I have made Thy name known to them, and will make it known; that the love wherewith Thou didst love Me may be in them, and I in them" (John 17:26). His love is to be made known continually through you and me. It can only be made known as we walk in loving obedience in every conversation and action. But what joy we experience when God is made known to others in our daily living!

As I studied these profound and moving verses, a resolve to love was taking form in me: *Lord, I resolve to love with your love no matter what my emotions may be saying.* Loving with his love began by my making a choice. The resolve to love is a foundational choice one must make on this love journey. Going deeper, I discovered I must also make the choice to love each time I was confronted with making a response to any situation in which I found myself. In every transaction, conversation or interaction I must out of my will commit myself again to love with God's love. My willful choice must be to will the will of God in each and every circumstance. I bring to death any selfish emotions and all they tell me to do or say. Now instead, I choose out of my will to obey his love commandment. A crossroads in my spiritual life has been reached with the dawning realization that I must take seriously the love commandment. Such a realization establishes me in a new dimension of grace and power.

While I was processing what God had been teaching me about my will and his love, I began to make a discovery. To my surprise, at least in the early stages of decision-making, my real choice, that is to love, was the opposite of my emotions. My emotions had ruled for so long that they were like the Sea of Galilee during a bad storm. Gradually they began to get the idea I was determined to move out of love and not out of my controlling emotions.

This decision making process caused a three-step pattern or formula to emerge. I like to call it "love processing." It is an internal process which is present at every decision-making point. At the outset I struggled with it because my selfish emotional response was always justifying itself. With continued practice this formula has become a natural part of my processing habits and takes only seconds to complete.

The formula is initiated at the outset of a situation by my hearing. The Holy Spirit poses a question, "Are you going to love with his love right now in this situation? What are you going to do now? Are you going to love? Are you going to act out God's attitudes, words and actions?"

The questions are the introduction to the following divine formula:

Step 1. I have the choice to love in this episode.

a. My will takes the initiative to do right as opposed to the stirred-up emotions such as anger or fear.

b. I lay down my emotions by turning from my self-life and its response to lash out in self-centeredness. Ephesians 4:22 or Luke 9:23.

c. I deny my old self-life which is not in character with God's love nature.

Step 2. I turn to Jesus and ask, "What would you have me do in this situation? I have chosen to love, regardless of the consequences."

a. Put on the new self, being like Christ.

b. Take up the cross. Ephesians 4:24. Luke 9:23.

Step 3. I am obedient to what God says to do or say.

a. "Follow me." Luke 9:23

b. Follow righteousness, holiness and truth. Ephesians 4:24.

I am strengthened each time I practice making a choice of my will to love, or as some people would say "taking up the cross." My will is strengthened for the good as I exercise it to do right. I believe divine love is released from the Holy Spirit by an act of my will. I resolve to allow that godly love to flow instead of venting my feelings.

This brief three-step response of love processing in answer to the Holy Spirit's question, "Are you going to love?" has now turned into a wonderful exercise. As my will is strengthened in the Love Exchange, it is more likely to say yes habitually.

Where I fail, I can still go God's way by owning up to my mistake, confessing, asking forgiveness and making restitution.

Does not Hebrews 5:14 say, "But solid food is for the mature, who because of practice have their senses trained to discern good and evil?" By exercising my will in making the right choice to love my spiritual senses become trained to discern good and evil.

God honors any effort on our part to love as Jesus loves. Such loving pleases him perhaps more than any prayer we pray, because our willingness to love as Jesus loves gives him access in that situation. God manifests himself in love because he is love. Even when I fail to love I can go back and make it right by means of confession, asking God and the person involved to forgive me. Illustrations of failures abound in all our lives.

Here is one episode where the three steps of this formula were actualized in a personal situation. My husband, John, and I were in the kitchen one morning following breakfast. As I put the dishes in the dish-washer, John made a comment that carried an edge which caused me to feel anger. The temptation came to make a defensive remark in return. The Lord said, "Are you resolved to love with my love in this situation?"

Incensed by this time, I was tempted to lash out at John. From my will however I said, "Lord I am resolved to love. I am making the choice to love with your love. What would you have me do?"

He answered, "Respond in love and patience. John is trying to say something to you, but you've been too busy and preoccupied to hear it. Ask him for what he has on his heart. Let him speak freely without interruption or justification on your part and receive it as from me."

All this took place in a few seconds. Turning to John I asked, "What is on your mind? You can tell me exactly what you mean. I know I've been too busy and preoccupied." Though the tone of my voice was loving, I still felt anger in my emotions. A wave of determination enabled me to cope with my screaming interior emotions. I vowed I would please my Father and give John a listening ear.

John opened his heart and shared his feelings concerning my preoccupation with others and clients and not leaving enough time for him. His observation was true. God's love enabled me to see John's situation and acknowledge the truth, although I'd felt anger at the beginning of the exchange. I denied my selfish emotions by laying down my self-life and opening myself to God's way of handling the situation. The result John and I experienced was his love working in both of us. Agreeing I would work on this area in my life, we embraced in a warm hug.

The final outcome of this entire scenario was threefold. First, I realized my need to improve my relationship with my husband. Because of resolving to love I was receptive and not defensive to what John said. Second, my husband was given an opportunity to express his feelings concerning an issue that needed to be resolved. God used this moment to deal with it because his timing was perfect. Third, and most important, this was a life-changing encounter for both of us. The sequence of events that morning was not merely to put a bandage on a festering wound that would need repeated attention later. Rather, what happened in the kitchen that morning brought a healing balm to what could have eventually been an impasse in our marriage. God administered love, bringing lasting results.

This resolution to love is not a denial of feelings. Because emotions are a natural part of our makeup they will be there. The important question is, "How are they handled in my life?" Paraphrased, Ephesians 4:26 summarizes this in by saying that we feel the emotion but do not sin against one another by letting that anger take over with damaging results.

I relate another experience of resolving to love as God has loved me. Listening to a client talk so warmly about a person who had been unloving to me, I thought, *You don't know that person like I do. I could change your mind about him in a minute.* Instantly the Holy Spirit questioned me, "Are you going to love in this instance? Are you resolved to love as you say you are?" Even though I felt anger in my emotions, I made the choice out of my will to love as God loves. When the woman finished talking, she did not know the spiritual processing I had been through. Within a few seconds I resolved to love and asked Jesus what he would have me do in this situation. What would be Jesus' response at this juncture?

The Holy Spirit said, "Agree that he is a wonderful man who loves me and wants to do right, then pray for him with this woman."

Following his admonition I began to pray. I sensed a love for that man I had never previously known. It was God's love and the Holy Spirit that prayed so intently for him. A few weeks later our paths crossed for the first time since that prayer experience, and for the first time there was Jesus' love between us. His loving and praying in me caused me to forgive totally, lay down the past and be free. We were relaxed with each other.

As we love, God frees us from our sins toward others. The exciting thing about such encounters is that when we resolve to obey the love commandments, God has a surprisingly unique reward—we are released, set free through obedience. As we obey the Holy Spirit when he reminds us of the divine formula in Matthew 5:44, prayer and love draw us into God's love for the people involved, and we are freed from loveless feelings.

When I began to cooperate with God by being obedient, he would speak of what he wanted me to do. I often needed to give myself some extended time in silence. During this time my will could gather energy to do what he had asked. It can safely be said that to say nothing was certainly a miracle in itself, for I have always considered my opinion of considerable value.

The challenge before us is to call forth the will when our emotions are so upset and angry. Just when we want to succumb to the flesh and vent our true feelings, God is asking us to make a life-changing decision. Do we explode and lose self control, or do we love and let God take control? With practice we become more proficient at holding our emotions in check and allowing the spirit of love to flow through our will. Soon it becomes fun to make the right choice.

As this resolve to love in all situations surfaced during the day I continued to practice the Love Exchange. The loving went on not only in my quiet time but throughout the day as well. Silently when necessary or out loud when possible in the home, car, department store or church, I was loving Jesus. My life became saturated with the love passages mentioned in Chapter 2.

The continual development of the Love Exchange takes it far beyond the quiet time. God wants it to become a moment-by-moment relationship with him.

When we are with others it becomes an ongoing love processing experience. While in solitude the Love Exchange is functioning, and we are being readied for the time of love processing. We long to please God by staying in his love, whether in moments of aloneness or in public. Resolving to obey the love commandments brings a deepening of his love in our lives and a growing love for him that releases answers to our prayers. His life-giving power begins to flow through us to others. God delivers love via his children and yearns to flood us with his love not only for ourselves but for others.

One afternoon during a break from my counseling activities, a friend called from her car while driving on the Pennsylvania Turnpike. Through most of her life she did not know God cared anything for her. In middle age she had experienced his love, but she needed to know that love in a more personal way. God had never manifested himself to her as she longed for him to do. During the last two years she had been involved in the Love Exchange and was thrilled with what was beginning to evolve. That day was no exception. As she was driving along she had been pouring out her love for God in the deepest way she had experienced yet. Suddenly she felt his wonderful presence with her in the car, and he began telling her how deeply he loved her. she knew deep in her heart what magnificent love he had for her. She was overflowing with his presence and love as we shared together the joy of that precious moment with him.

By now we may be asking, *but what if it fails? Isn't this only for those extraordinary people? It couldn't be for us because we have too many problems and pressures. Does this love business really work? Aren't there some situations beyond the love of God?*

137

The word of God says, "Love never fails," (1 Corinthians 13:8). God's love, divine love, never fails! We have seen it put into action so rarely, we do not believe his love never fails. I've never heard that text addressed. Why? Because its hard to believe it is true, and because we are so ashamed of our failures. Therefore, we push it aside and act like it doesn't matter. We know so little about his love we don't even know how often to release it!

When we are actually channels of his love, his love never fails. I believe this area of God's love, released by obedience to the love commandments and infused by the Love Exchange, is the arena of miracles, signs and wonders of which Jesus spoke. "Greater works than these shall he do" (John 14:12).

We try to live the Christian life solely out of human love, and it results in nothing but the up and down gamut of human emotions, unpredictable and totally insecure. Our Christian life is then at the mercy of human love, self-seeking and self-exalting. Our emotions become the controlling factors, not our will controlling us with a desire to love God in all situations, even if it means our human will being pushed into a more humble place than we would seek.

Having worked with this whole divine love experiment for many years now, I believe it as never before. The Christian life is God in me loving through me and submitting to that love. In the Love Exchange I find his love somehow encourages and fortifies my will to want to please him all the time, in all conversations and interactions with others. Is this not Philippians 2:13 at work? "For it is God who is at work in you, both to will and to work for his good pleasure." He alters my will by loving me unconditionally so that I yearn never to step outside that glorious love. My desire to please him is my will seeking to stay under the lordship of Christ and his love in all I do and say. How deeply I want to please him reveals how deeply I love him.

As God multiplies my love for him and his to me in the Love Exchange, my desire to please him becomes a passion. As each event presents itself in my day, I see these opportunities as his appointments to let me practice and exercise my obedience to his will.

Failures will always come when I do not maintain a deep love for my Beloved and want to please him. If I do not make it my chief aim in life to stay in his love whatever the price; if I do not take the high road of obedience and make the choice out of my will to love; if I give in to my emotions and demand my rights, my way, my justification—then there is no way love can help me or anyone else in a given situation. The tragedy is that since God must flow through me, if I refuse to allow him passage into the situation, he may well be blocked if no one else is going the way of divine love. Many times I may well be the only vessel God has to disclose his wonderful love. 1 John 4:19 says, "We love, because He first loved us."

Dr. Tom Carruth, a long time friend says, "I want to be the first to love in any situation since he was the first to love." I love that statement. Are you and I the first to love in all situations?

The hard cruel reality is that if I spend no time in the presence of my Beloved, so I can partake of his love nature, then I will take the low road of human love and will surely fail. Human love has a hard time seeing its sins and mistakes, and it loves to blame the other person. I believe divine love, or Calvary love as many greater saints have expressed it, is willing to take all the blame as he did on the cross.

Even though I have failed his wondrous love on numerous occasions, the glorious fact remains that by choosing God's love, even when I fail, I can step back into that love through repentance, confession and restitution. I will hurry back to do whatever is needed to abide once again in his love, because "The one who does not love does not know God, for God is love (1 John 4:8). In other words, when I choose not to love with his love, at that time and place I step out of his love and the experience of knowing him. He can only be known in love since he *is* love.

Two experiences come to mind: one of my failures and one failure of a friend.

When the Lord had spoken to me about laying aside my musical gift so that I might be full time in the life of prayer, the response from many friends was not very enthusiastic. One dear friend let me know frequently that my choice could not possibly be of God. Cynthia is a godly woman and someone I deeply respect, but I felt in my heart she was mistaken. I appreciated how she felt, but she made walking in my decision to follow God's calling difficult. One day she started at me again about my decision. I came to the end of my resources. My anger flared within, and I told her coldly but nicely that she knew nothing about God's orders for me. Cynthia then replied, "He can't have you abandon your gift so totally."

I saw that she did not understand my position, so we dropped it. However, I let my anger take root and made up my mind not to be around her much. I rationalized this by thinking I was letting her cool off a bit, but actually I was the one who needed to cool off. I needed to have spoken the truth but in love and not anger. It was not easy for me to steer clear of her, especially in prayer settings, because our paths crossed so often.

Seeing her in a room with other people, I would be too busy to talk with her should the occasion present itself.

The Love Exchange was not quite as meaningful for several days following this incident. I thought that I must be too tired to pray or involve myself in the Love Exchange. After several days of this nothingness I found myself saying to the Lord, "I'm too busy, too pushed, Lord, sorry. I am here, but too much is going on in my mind."

Realizing a deeper issue was involved here, I saw my need to go deeper with the Lord. The deeper issue was that often others, even long-time friends and family members, have not heard the message of God for us. Since they do not fully understand, the degree of understanding they exhibit must not defuse or affect our love from the outside.

A week later the Lord finally got my attention. "What are you going to do about Cynthia? You cannot continue to avoid her as you wait for something to happen in your relationship."

"Lord, I am only waiting for her to cool off." I was feeling guilty and a bit squeamish.

"Where are you functioning outside of my love?"

"I love her, I just don't want anything to do with her!"

"You call that my love?"

"No, I know that is wrong, but she has tried my soul."

"What are you going to do about it? It's causing problems between you and me."

"I don't want anything or anybody between us. I can't stand it." I asked him then what I should have asked a week ago, "Lord, what would you have me do?"

"Tell Cynthia you must talk with her today and take the whole blame as I took the whole blame for you on the cross. Then you ask her forgiveness and release her to be who she is whether she understands or not."

"Lord, I ask you to forgive my sin in anger and impatience and shutting down in retaliation to her. I will confess today to her, assuming the whole blame."

As I met with Cynthia and began to ask her forgiveness, saying it was all my fault and meaning it, she broke in and wanted to take the whole blame too. We threw our arms around one another and love once again never failed!

The force of retaliation is strong, but we can return to God's love through repentance, confession and obedience. I realize that many times God's divine love may take a long time to work in another's heart. But as we confess and ask the person to forgive us, we are acting out God's love. Their response is their business. No matter whether they receive it or not, I am being obedient to the Lord of love.

The other example concerns a young businessman who was earnestly seeking to walk in the Love Exchange. Jim was giving God twenty to twenty-five minutes each morning with some time for the exchange.

As he worked successfully in the firm to which he belonged, he sought to stay in God's love all through the day. Though all kinds of difficulties came his way, such as jealousy over his success and anger because things seemed to go well for him, he stayed in God's love and was able to return only God's love for good.

Something always happened, however, when all the employees would meet in the conference room for their weekly meeting. This meeting was a time for each man to share the things that were important to his work and how it related to the others' work. This young man, who had been God's man for the occasion in so many one-on-one situations, now became almost like a different person. With every barb that came his way he found himself unable to stay in God's love. His response became defensive, angry and egocentric. He defended his place and his rights, sometimes in inappropriate ways. He could handle his fellow employees one by one, but as they came together, all his desire to obey the love commandments was lost.

This unreasonable behavior went on for several months, with this young businessman in total confusion. He left those meetings in absolute disgust with himself, feeling totally defeated and so discouraged he thought of ditching his quiet time with God. The Love Exchange certainly was not working for him in a corporate setting. He felt his witness on a one-to-one basis was totally nonauthentic because he sabotaged his witness when he was in a group.

"What a failure. Must not be much to this whole thing," he muttered to God one day. "I can't do it. What is going on anyway? I've failed to love, and I am so distressed at what comes out of me. I act like I don't even belong to you, Lord."

"I still love you as you are," was God's response. "Tell me how you feel, and I'm going to love you whether you succeed or not."

"I don't see how you can," he replied.

"I do, just relax now, take a big breath and know I love you."

As this man got quiet and relaxed in God' presence, the Lord said, "You want to know what's happening. Do you want to know badly enough to change?"

"Yes, Lord, I don't want to fail you this way anymore. What's going on?"

"Your growth with me is not far enough along yet for you to take such an aggressive role with everyone present. You feel too threatened, so you slip out of my love to fight your own battles the old way. Your self-life says, 'Hey, I'm important; I'm doing great. I demand you notice me and give me my strokes.' From now on, assume a much more quiet, humble role. Don't give your opinion until you have been asked, and then stay in my love by preferring others above yourself. Stay humble in my presence and theirs. Pray with love all the time these weekly meetings are in session. You do not need to defend yourself; only show love. Lay the defense of your importance down at the foot of the cross. Do you understand?"

"Yes, Lord, thank you. I've always wanted everyone to like me. forgive me. I'll keep my mouth shut more."

It was pretty tough going for awhile, being more silent and not drawing attention to himself. The others would look over at him and expect him to fight, but he would only smile and pray. Slowly, ever so slowly, he got his self-life under the control of his will and God's love.

He began to experience peace, the byproduct of love, and found the meetings were wonderful times to obey Matthew 5:44—pray and love, love and pray. The spirit of Jesus was more evident in him, and his mouth and heart were more under God's loving control.

The miraculous thing about the Love Exchange is the tremendous change God brings about within the subterranean levels of our loves. As God loves us, he is remodeling us and our attitudes. We are to be so knit to Jesus that our love and life become one. Are you knit to him? It is a knitting together as 1 Samuel 18:1 describes the relationship between David and Jonathan.

Jesus said in Matthew 22:37-40, "'You shall love the Lord your God with all your heart, and with all your soul, and with all your mind.' This is the great and foremost commandment. The second is like it, 'You shall love your neighbor as yourself.'" On these two commandments depend the whole Law and the Prophets."

The love commandments can be summarized in these two great commandments—loving God and loving people.

ಞ•ಚೀ

One of the most
thrilling effects
of the Love Exchange
is that my self-focus is shifted,
as I begin to see things
more from God's
point of view.

ಞ•ಚೀ

Chapter 7

The Love Exchange Becomes the Exchanged Life

"Love is patient, love is kind, and is not jealous; love does not brag and is not arrogant, does not act unbecomingly; it does not seek its own, is not provoked, does not take into account a wrong suffered, does not rejoice in unrighteousness, but rejoices with the truth; bears all things, believes all things, hopes all things, endures all things. Love never fails. . . . "
1 Corinthians 13:4-8a

The lovely autumn afternoon was fading into the sunset hour when I pulled my car out of the parking lot at Asbury College and headed toward home. I had begun praying the minute I got behind the wheel—for I had seen the Holy Spirit do a wonderful job of assuring a young student of the fact that God truly loved him. My student had been sharing with me his joy, centered on experiences of the Love Exchange, and to my delight

God had given this young man a real sense of his eternal caring for him.

Reflecting on this scenario I began audibly pouring out my love to God. My stream of love centered on telling him how much I appreciated the way he revealed his love through his Word to my student. My heart leaped up to God in such love and gratitude for his great faithfulness, his great Fatherly love, his compassion. As I reviewed all that he had done for me and was currently doing, my love for him literally shot out beyond vocabulary and my deepest feelings. An overwhelming love for him flooded my spirit as simultaneously I felt pain in my heart for him for my love went so deep.

"Lord, you are something else. I cannot even express how much I love you. No language can touch what my heart feels toward you. You are so precious to me. How I love you."

Before I could finish loving and thanking him I began to experience in my heart a deep sense of his love for me. As God began to pour out his love for me I heard his assurance, "You are precious to me and I love you." I sensed a deep reality of his love. This touch of assurance increased my love for him.

So fulfilling was this Love Exchange as we rode together that we spent several minutes in a deep communion of heart to heart. 1 Corinthians 6:17 was true. "The one who joins himself to the Lord is one spirit with Him." I felt such a oneness with him, I expressed my feelings of love in a wordless vocabulary.

Suddenly, in the midst of that deep and exhilarating Love Exchange, the Holy Spirit clearly spoke to me about prayer for a certain young man for whom I had been praying for several years. His needs were both spiritual and deeply emotional.

"Lord, I don't want to pray for anyone right now. I want only to love you and bask in your presence. I'll do the praying later on."

Actually, I did not want to remove myself in any way from Jesus, but rather to draw closer to him, to rest in him and abide in him. This was the most precious Love Exchange I had yet experienced, and I wanted nothing to interrupt or intrude on this sacred time.

He said, "I understand, but what are we going to do with all this love?"

"What do you mean, Lord?" I questioned.

"Would it not be a shame not to send it to someone who needs it today?"

"Can we do that, Jesus?" I questioned?

"Yes, let's send our mingled love out to Sid. I want to send my love and heal him today," came the response.

Dr. Glen Clark had taught for years in the Camps Farthest Out that prayer is potent when we send out our love mingled with God's love. I had experienced that before in corporate prayer group situations, but never only the Lord and me. With this experience all that Dr. Clark had taught had real meaning. With a change of attitude I gladly replied, "Lord, I'll do whatever you want. Flow through me to this desperate young man. Minister your love through me and we will send out healing love—now."

The intensity of God's love was so strong I was shaking as I prayed for this young man. The prayer was a pure love prayer.

"Heavenly Father, send your eternal, holy, restoring love to Sid. Pour out yourself and your love on him right now, no matter where he is or what he is doing. Manifest yourself to him today as you bring him into your presence. Let him cross the line into wholeness and completely surrender himself to you." I felt the intensity of that prayer then slip out beyond vocabulary. I only experienced encompassing love for God and Sid.

My heart felt as if it were bursting with God's love for Sid, and deep in my spirit I knew my prayer had been answered. What a glorious experience to partake of God's marvelous love and know that the promise, "Love never fails" (1 Corinthians 13:8) is true. We often fail to exhibit God's love, but his kind of love never fails.

As I pulled into our driveway, dusk had turned into darkness, and as I opened the back door the phone was ringing. My intuition indicated that it would be Sid on the phone and it was. He could hardly speak he was so excited. He had had a wondrous time of experientially knowing that God loves him! God had poured out himself in such a way that Sid was flooded with the reality of how much God cared. The reality of this love empowered him in wholeness that day in a deeper dimension than ever before. In fact, he spoke to me the words of the prayer the Holy Spirit had prayed through me. This became the avenue whereby his desperately needed healing was realized.

Sid needed to make a righteous decision that very day for God and he said, "Margaret, if God loves me so much, as he has shown me today, I will show my love for him and be obedient. I am going with God today because of his total love for me. I must do it today. I have said a total yes to him. I've never known his love as I have known it today. He is wonderful."

Great joy and excitement consumed me, but I was not surprised. I had not a shadow of a doubt, for what had transpired was authentic and firmly fixed. This man continues to walk in great victory four years later. He is an avid intercessor and has a great heart for prayer.

We may ask, "Isn't this potent business?" Yes, God's love is mighty potent! Isn't this what intercession is all about? Isn't intercession our picking up on his heart and mind by being close to God, by hearing who it is he wants to pray for through us? These prayers are always answered because the Holy Spirit prays only the will of God for his glory.

Let us examine more closely what happened here. First, a brief historical background. For centuries in the school of prayer there have been two camps. In one camp are those who feel intercession is the only way to pray. The other camp is composed of those who have felt that contemplation is the only prayer form with power.

Contemplation has been criticized for being smug, an intimate "God and me" relationship that excludes everything but my little world. Such an attitude generates a feeling of letting the rest of the world go by. While we are on the Mount of Transfiguration, if you will, those in the valley are of no concern.

While contemplation is criticized for excluding the world's needs, intercessors are criticized for not being interested in God except for what he can do *for us*.

My consensus is that it is not intercession vs. contemplation, but rather the blending of the two prayer experiences.

The manifestation of this blended prayer experience could begin with the Love Exchange. As I move closer to God in this exchange he is allowed to bring to my recollection the subjects for my prayer at this time. His concerns become my concerns. This then becomes intercession in the purest form. It is God-originated, God-inspired, God-prayed and God fulfilling his need for that time through me, his vessel. It is the wordless loving experience in the Love Exchange that is paralleled in the intercession experience where the Holy Spirit yearns inexpressibly as he intercedes on behalf of a person or situation.

In this most complete form of praying there is a basic characteristic common to the Love Exchange and intercession. The commonality is that we love so deeply that we move out beyond what words can express. It becomes the groanings or the inexpressible yearnings of love that we find in Romans 8:26.

How often have parents found themselves with feelings of such love for their children they are totally speechless in trying to pray for them! They only feel the power of their love beyond any verbiage. I believe those feelings beyond any articulation are powerful. Is this not the yearning of Jesus over Jerusalem? Deep prayer is wordless yearnings over God and those for whom we pray. After all our vocabularies are very limited, "but the heart has reasons the mind knows not," says Pascal.

In both experiences of contemplation and intercession there is a self-forgetfulness. In the Love Exchange or contemplation I am focused more on God while forgetting myself. In intercession it is an identification with the person or situation as I forget about myself.

Rest assured, however, that all experiences will not be as dramatic or instantaneous as related in the example of Sid. When the Holy Spirit's love is released within us, he prays God's prayers for those whom God desires in his own fashion and according to his schedule. God will act, but how and when he desires. I do believe that as the body of Christ moves into more allegiance to loving him with all of our hearts and obey the love commandments, we will indeed have more instantaneous answers to prayer.

Therefore, at the height of the Love Exchange it is my personal experience that at numerous times God will bring to our minds and hearts those persons he holds in love needing Holy Spirit prayer in that very moment. Out of the apex of the Love Exchange comes God-directed intercession. How much more this is God-directed and God-fulfilled praying than our more common intercession when we find ourselves overwhelmed by prayer requests. We often feel intercession for so many needs is one more burden of prayer we must carry. Our intercession comes out of the flesh and brings the fleshly reward—nothing (John 6:63)!

Clarification should be made at this point concerning prayer lists. They are a useful tool of prayer for many people. The Holy Spirit can certainly empower the praying for everyone on the list. But more significantly, when we are seeking to live all through the day in the Love Exchange, God can access our minds and hearts at any time with the many persons for whom we will pray. He quickens the Holy Spirit in us to pray God's will for those he causes us to remember. Praying therefore becomes a laying down of our life, for his life to be activated in us in prayer. 1 John 3:16 says, "We know love by this, that He laid down His life for us; and we ought to lay down our lives for the brethren."

In the Love Exchange, God gets the attention of our hearts and brings the people to us he yearns over and then we pray over these at a specific time and place. So much of intercession can be little more than our trying to tell him who needs prayer and our praying the prayer. When we no longer administer the directives to God concerning the prayer request of intercession, a real miracle can take place in the Love Exchange. Such intercession, which is birthed in the mutual love of the Love Exchange, is the Holy Spirit praying God's prayers in God's way for God's glory.

What I believe actually happens in the Love Exchange is that I am nurtured and cared for, and so I am no longer pushing my prayers, my will or my way on the Lord during my prayer time. Because my needs are met, he can care for others through me. God can take over this request and do as he sees best in praying. He does the praying for the right reasons in the right way.

How do we move into greater intimacy with God? First, by beginning to move into the truth of Romans 8:26 initiated by our Love Exchange. A friendship of close sharing develops when God opens up his heart and purpose to us. He draws us into an ever deepening relationship where through my heart and mind, his Spirit flows in intercession for others.

A second way we develop on this ongoing friendship is by moving from the Love Exchange into the Ex-changed Life.

Historically the experience of the Exchanged Life is a term used by early Christian writers and goes back to our wonderful Lord's saying in John 5:19-20, "The Son can do nothing of Himself, unless it is something He sees the Father doing, for whatever the Father does, these things the Son also does in like manner. For the Father loves the Son, and shows Him all things that He himself is doing; and greater works than these will He show Him that you may marvel." Jesus goes on to say, "I can do nothing on My own initiative" (v. 30), and "The Father abiding in Me does his works" (John 14:10b).

Jesus experienced God's life in him, doing God's works. It is the Holy Spirit in us that is to do Jesus' works in us. Paul says this in his letter to the Galatians: 2:20. "I have been crucified with Christ; and it is no longer I who live, but Christ lives in me; and the life which I now live in the flesh I live by faith in the Son of God, who loved me, and delivered Himself up for me."

We are to decrease in the amount of selfish control we have over our lives. Simultaneously God takes more control and dominion over our surrendered lives. The Love Exchange allows him entrance into more of me, enabling his love to bring changes in my will, my self-love. The Exchanged Life today is still the same as it had been when Jesus said it was the Father in him doing God's works, for he took no initiative in anything.

Jesus can be allowed into my life more and more only as I love him more and give him permission to take over in my life and do what he needs to do at all times.

I experienced a concrete example of this while in a northern community. For three days I had had a full schedule as the speaker at a prayer conference, including the regular commitment of bringing the messages and several appointments for counseling. It had been an intense three days, and I needed rest. How I looked forward to the fourth day, intended as a day for relaxing. But God knew what I did not know. He knew of two women who needed his help, and he was placing them directly in my path, one which would take up the morning and one which would take up the afternoon.

I would have enjoyed a day of sightseeing, but deeper was the desire to love God by pleasing him. He asked me to lay down my plans and let him do what he wanted to do for these women. It would take my cooperation in joyful surrender. I loved him so fully that I allowed him to live his life through me, rather than living out my personal desires. Help that was desperately needed was brought to these women, and I knew the joy of the Love Exchange and the Exchanged Life as well.

Probably one of the most thrilling effects of the Love Exchange is that my self-focus is shifted, as I begin to see things more from God's point of view. Because I am growing daily in loving him more fully, he begins to share with me his intense love for others and his world. He also deepens my concern and love for his world. My self-preoccupation with prayer concerns for myself, my family and my church began to fade into the background as I was flooded with God's occupation for his world. Yes, there are times when my own needs are a part of my prayers, but now because they are a part of his world not because they are top priority with me. As a child experiences the world of walking instead of crawling, I began to experience his love for his world. He yearns again through me, in deep prayer groanings of love, for Jerusalem, New York, Los Angeles, Lexington. He prays through me for world leaders and authorities that "entreaties and prayers, petitions and thanksgivings, be made on behalf of all men, for kings and all who are in authority, in order that we may lead a tranquil and quiet life in all godliness and dignity" (1 Timothy 2:1-2).

The Love Exchange produces a life exchange. A metamorphosis takes place as I move from an unattractive self-centered creature to a godly creature where God quickens in me his life of unselfish sacrificial loving and praying. The Exchanged Life even causes me some pain when I want to do what is pleasing to me rather than giving him full expression.

Once the metamorphosis has taken place how do we grow in greater intimacy with God? The Love Exchange is one powerful device of God to conform us to the image of Jesus. His divine love releases his nature through me and bonds me in ever increasing intimacy to him. The Psalmist affirms this with, "I will be satisfied with Thy likeness when I awake" (Psalm 17:15).

As I experience even a fraction of God's love for me in the Love Exchange I am encouraged to trust him more. The more I release myself to him in a growing surrender the greater intimacy I experience. He has increasing control over my will and empowers that will to move in loving obedience to his love commandments and nature.

As the child learning to walk does not want to crawl, so we, when we begin to experience his love, want no longer to crawl. Now that we have experienced the Love Exchange we want to walk in the Love Exchange, which is walking in the Exchanged Life. In three passages of Scripture Paul affirms us in this.

1 John 3:2, 3: "Beloved, now we are the children of God and it has not appeared as yet what we shall be. We know that, when He appears, we shall be like Him, because we shall see Him as He is. And everyone who has this hope fixed on Him purifies himself, just as He is pure."

Ephesians 5:1-2a: "Therefore be imitators of God, as beloved children; and walk in love, just as Christ also loved you, and gave himself up for us."

1 John 3:18: "Little children, let us not love with word or with tongue, but in deed and truth." Our hearts are holy, or whole, when we walk in his redemptive love and allow that love to manifest itself in the world through us. The Love Exchange is one way to do this.

1 Thessalonians 3:12-13 "And may the Lord cause you to increase and abound in love for one another, and for all men, just as we also do for you; so that He may establish your hearts unblamable in holiness before our God and Father at the coming of our Lord Jesus with all His saints."

As the Love Exchange is pursued, his life of healing love will be manifested more and more in us. There is a fountain of God's love where we may drink, and with even a small amount of love in us he begins to flow out to his world. Are you drinking daily of those wondrous waters of love? Jesus said, "Everyone who drinks of this water shall thirst again; by whoever drinks of the water that I shall give him shall never thirst; but the water that I shall give him shall become in him a well of water springing up to eternal life" (John 4:13, 14).

I believe this is the "high road" of which John Wesley spoke centuries ago. If you want adventure, challenge and real growth in a deeply satisfying intimacy with

God, take the high road of the Love Exchange, which opens into the Exchanged Life.

My deepest prayer for you is that you open your heart to a growing intimacy of his love shed abroad in your heart by the Holy Spirit (Romans 5:5).

What is the Love Exchange?

1. It is a prayer model, an exercise or pattern God gave me as a means of opening my spirit and my mind to God so he can communicate his love to me as I meditate on his words of love to me from the Word of God.

2. It is a way of learning to be more responsive and receptive to his love nature.

3. It is an opening of myself to practice an attitude of trust toward God, through believing more and more that he does truly love me. Galatians 5:6 says faith works through love. As I see and experience his total acceptance of me, I learn I can have faith in him.

4. It is training of every part of me, particularly my real self, to believe what God says about me in the Bible as in John 3:16 and 1 John 4:16.

5. It is a concrete pattern whereby I cooperate with God, in a definite time and place, by saying yes to his love nature, allowing him to meet the deepest needs of my real self by being loved by him.

6. It is the beginning of a love journey of being transformed into the image of Jesus, where God's eternal

love work becomes the mark of my life, as it was in Jesus' life.

7. It enables me to take Jesus' words concerning the love commandments seriously and begin to allow him to teach me about his divine love.

What the Love Exchange is Not

1. It is not the guarantee of a quickie fix or cure to all my emotional or spiritual ills. It is not a shortcut to avoid pain or the cross of Jesus Christ. In reality, the Love Exchange brings us to real love, Calvary love, and reveals what the cross means in our love life. It is not a detour from reality or to bring us into spiritual places we are totally unprepared to receive.

2. It is not a flight from self-knowledge or avoiding seeing myself as I am. Rather God's love, and his love alone, empowers me to see myself and yet not despair. It is a journey into ever deepening self-knowledge.

3. It is not a substitute for facing my emotional and mental problems, i.e., mental illness or neurosis. It takes reasonable, relatively whole mental health to participate in any interaction or exchange in an honest way.

4. If we are moving in any out-and-out disobedience to God, the Love Exchange will be an impossibility. There must be a deeper sincerity to want to do right, or else the pattern is a sham.

5. It could be misunderstood by people with emotional hang-ups, who want their sensualities, their imaginations and ego needs to be caught up in a fantasy realm. God will seek to draw us away from "spiritualizing" or rhapsodizing over experiences that are false. Our ego needs to be accepted, approved and, importantly, handled honestly and in a real way.

I know a woman with tremendous ego needs who felt the Love Exchange would get for her all that had been denied in her life. She wanted to get on a "spiritual" journey to control and manipulate God. This, of course, is impossible. Our need for control prevents God's love from taking control of us. God began to deal with her not only in the Love Exchange but in professional counseling, and she realized she must lay down her agenda and release God to work on the issues he felt must be tackled first. The Love Exchange has grown in meaning as she has become more in touch with her own feelings and needs.

6. The Love Exchange released me from being a super Christian, for he understands my humanity. I can be where I am and who I am with God. Psalm 103:13-14 says, "Just as a father has compassion on his children, so the Lord has compassion on those who fear Him. For He Himself knows our frame; He is mindful that we are but dust."

When I am too exhausted and over-extended, too busy running here and there, any quiet relaxed time with God is difficult. It will take some time to focus on him and gather myself with all my scatteredness. These times will be more difficult to move into heartfelt loving him. I may have anger and resentment that needs to be dealt with first. I can relax with God and allow him to deal with all my needs. The Love Exchange produces a deepening honesty with myself and God.

Paul sweeps into 1 Corinthians by saying in chapter 12, verse 31: "And I show you a still more excellent way"—the way of God's wondrous, divine love. He reaches the climax of that chapter in verse 8: "Love never fails."

He waits for you in the journey of the Love Exchange. Will you meet God there?